A FALSE STROKE OF GENIUS

THE WAYNE LARKINS STORY

Wayne Larkins in the veteran stage of his playing career.

A FALSE STROKE OF GENIUS

THE WAYNE LARKINS STORY

John Wallace

TEMPUS

First published 2001

Published by:
Tempus Publishing Limited
The Mill, Brimscombe Port
Stroud, Gloucestershire, GL5 2QG

Typesetting and origination by Tempus Publishing Ltd.
Printed and bound in Great Britain

British Library Cataloguing in Publication Data.
A catalogue record for this book is available from the British Library

ISBN 07524 2166 2

Contents

FOREWORD

I was delighted to be asked to write the foreword to the biography of my old friend and colleague at Northampton, Wayne Larkins. When I joined the County in 1978 Wayne, affectionately known as 'Ned' on the county circuit, was really starting to show his skills as an opening batsman and a particularly fine player of fast bowling.

We were colleagues for six seasons in a team which enjoyed considerable success, due in no small measure to Wayne's aggressive batting which, in conjunction with the likes of Allan Lamb, Peter Willey, Geoff Cook and Richard Williams, often instilled the fear into other counties' bowlers of being 'thunderbatted.' Many was the time that he wrested the initiative from the opposition by his quickness of foot and exciting stroke play. The fact that England's Test team availed itself so little of his enormous talent remains a mystery to many people and these thirteen appearances in his country's colours do him scant justice.

A genuinely lovable character, Wayne loves the game and continues to play cricket for Bedfordshire at an age when many others have put their bats and their pads away, so, sadly, I see him rarely these days. When our paths do cross, however, I remember with great affection and no little admiration our days together as colleagues in the Northamptonshire team.

Tim Lamb
Chief Executive, England and Wales Cricket Board
2001

PREFACE

In the middle of the 1970s I was reading my usual cricket column when I saw the name of Wayne Larkins mentioned as a potential England prospect. Could anyone really be named in such an avant-garde fashion? Had his mother been a follower of the hero of *Red River* or his father a brewer or was I just unfamiliar with the new vogue of Christian names? There had to be a reason. I became fascinated and gradually started to follow the fortunes of the good Wayne. Very little happened for a year or two, just a few good scores for Northants, and I suppose my interest may well have slackened a little. Then, in 1979, I saw him selected to tour Australia and everything perked up a little, but since it was a crucial time in my own career, I failed to give the matter the attention it clearly deserved and it was not until one Sunday afternoon in 1983 that I became focused once more. I had enjoyed my Sunday lunch and had the choice of mowing the lawn or watching some cricket on BBC2, which used at that time to be a feature of many cricket lovers' week-ends but which nowadays, sadly, gives way to ping-pong or the triple jump. Predictably, the cricket won. What was on in the John Player League? Yes, Northants were playing Warwickshire, it was probably worth a look. Where's Wardown Park, I thought? Luton? I didn't know they played cricket there. It's a long way from Lord's or Hove, where I usually watch cricket. Don't they make Vauxhall cars there?

The thought of the assembly line was soon transferred into a picture of cricketing beauty. Wayne Larkins enacted a controlled massacre of the visitors' attack. There was no slogging, no hoicks over mid-wicket, but cool, calm aggression which caused the Northants total to increase inexorably but with apparently little effort. Bailey went for 27, Peter Willey came in and enjoyed the fun, making 84, and Wayne went smoothly on and on and on. At 298 for 2 the slaughter came to a close and Wayne strolled off nonchalantly with an undefeated 172. There would have been no point in watching any further cricket that afternoon: it would have made me feel that I had come down to earth again. I drank my cup of tea and the lawn did get cut after all.

When I recounted what I had seen to my cricketing friends, I was keen to tell them, of course, how I had always rated Wayne – they nodded politely as friends do, but not much more was said. In most of my cricketing conversations the name of Wayne Larkins occurred regularly, but nobody seemed particularly interested. 'He's the fellow who went out to South Africa and got banned, isn't he?' I'd reply: 'Yes, that's right, but he's a really great batsman as I have been telling you all along.' Time passed, but my interest remained and I felt triumphant when the selectors recalled him in 1986. I was, however, the butt of some amusement with my friends because his average was seven point something at that time and, in any event, he didn't play because he had managed to break a finger yet again. It was not, in fact, until 1989 that I was vindicated by The Nehru Cup and the West Indies tour – I was right after all, especially when the Aussies were hit for six at Hyderabad.

My stock began to rise a little, especially as Wayne played rather well in the Caribbean. In the following season he was again unable to keep his fingers out of the way of rising cricket balls, so he did not get a chance that summer, but, of course, I continued to advance his name for the Australian tour and the selectors apparently heard me – or was it just Graham Gooch they heard? A colleague accused me of being the secretary of the WLPS – the Wayne Larkins Preservation Society. From then on, I have had my ups and downs. Up, when I read headlines like 'Larkins and Gower hold up the Australians' – I had to be right, didn't I? Down? I guess it's been a bit downhill ever since.

When I was about to retire I knew, however, that I had to write the biography of the great man. He had been sacked, apparently unjustly, from Durham, so I wrote to him and commiserated. He did not reply, because he never does, but Debbie, his partner, did ring up and showed some interest.

Since undertaking this project, I have discovered that its subject is, as one might perhaps expect, not always the easiest man to get in touch with; a planned meeting at The George at Stamford lacked Wayne's presence (although he was ready with a swift apology) while most correspondence went unanswered. I finally met him when his contract with Durham had not been renewed and he was in the Bedfordshire side playing at Fenners in Cambridge. When I arrived Wayne was fielding and apparently dropping a few catches at slip from the snippets I picked up from the pavilion chatter. As he came up the stairs from the dressing rooms into the lunch room, I was at the top and ready to pounce. He looked shy and surprised. 'John?' he asked diffidently. The destroyer of a thousand bowlers was really a very modest chap. We talked a little in the dressing room, as he told the skipper that the press were there. 'I don't mind missing a bit of fielding,' he said with a schoolboyish smile. My schoolmasterly questions seemed at times to intimidate him, but what I learned about him I liked tremendously.

My next assignation had to be in his back yard, Wantage Road, the home of Northants cricket, at 11 o'clock one November morning. My own train to Northampton was slightly late and I was ready with my apologies. I need not perhaps have worried as Wayne did not arrive for another hour-and-a-half, but I had the good fortune to encounter David Capel, who assured me that this display of tardiness was quite normal. David and I enjoyed a marvellous chat, and I am grateful indeed for all the help he has given me with this biography.

I have had little success arranging to meet Wayne since then. Indeed I have phoned Sedgefield and Leamington Spa so many times for snippets of information that BT must be thinking of asking me to join the Board. I was once about to board a train in Tunbridge Wells for a further meeting in Northampton, only to find out at the last minute that he was still in bed in Sedgefield. Few people are more elusive.

I did, however, meet him once more, when he was playing for Bedfordshire at Dunstable on a bright Sunday morning. He seemed pre-occupied. Was it that the ball that bowled him had kept unsportingly low? I don't know. He couldn't say much, he was thinking about the game. 'I'll write it all down for you, though, and send it by post.' I'm still waiting for it, of course, and my stamped envelopes are doubtless still sitting somewhere in their pristine state. For all that, I have met many marvellous people in the course of my travels. It has been a labour of love, but my goodness, what a labour!

ACKNOWLEDGEMENTS

My thanks are due to Geoffrey Moorhouse for allowing me to quote from *The Best Loved Game* (Hodder and Stoughton), to Simon Hughes for his permission to include a short piece from *A Lot of Hard Yakka* (Headline), to Jack Bannister for the quotations from the Wayne Larkins section of *The Innings of my Life* (Headline), to the *Northampton Chronicle & Echo* for the use of their library files and photographs and the *Newcastle Chronicle & Journal* for supplying cuttings.

I am deeply grateful to all the following for their help in advising me on matters of publication, style and cricket facts, sparing time for interviews and reading through the text: James Howarth, my publisher, Keith Andrew, Brian Barron for the use of Wayne Larkins' benefit brochure, Julian Baskcomb, Mike Brearley, Dennis Brookes, David Capel, Geoff Cook for the notes which comprise Chapter 13, Stephen Coverdale, Ray East, Matthew Engel, Doug Ferguson, Graeme Fowler, John Fowling, Mike Gatting, Graham Gooch, Michael Green, Jim Hawkins, Alan Hodgson, David and Audrey Hoare for their welcome to Bedfordshire CCC, Tony Kingston (Northamptonshire CCC scorer) for the scoresheets of Wayne Larkins' most famous innings, Allan Lamb, Tim Lamb for writing the foreword, the late Mavis Larkins, Melvin Larkins, John Lever, Debbie Lines, Ann Long, Ian Lucas, Chris McCooey for proof-reading the text, Mushtaq Mohammad, Brian Odell, Richard Peel, Bill Peet, Andrew Radd, Derek Randall, Tim Rich, George and Audrey Sharp, Will Stapleton, David Steele, Chris Tavaré, Chris Utting, Jim Watts, Chris White for advice on style, Peter Willey, David Wilson, and, last but certainly not least, my wife Anne for her constant advice and encouragement.

I am also grateful to Northamptonshire County Cricket Club for the use of their interview and office facilities at Wantage Road.

The following are acknowledged for the use of photographs in this book: All Sport, Graham Alsop, David Capel, John Courtney, George Herringshaw (*www.sporting-heroes.net*), the late Mavis Larkins, Debbie Lines, Graham and Diana Morris, David Munden, Bill Smith, and Bob Thomas (Popperfoto).

INTRODUCTION

'He was more naturally gifted than any batsman in the land, and no attack escaped his power' is how Simon Hughes, cricketer, author and commentator, saw Wayne Larkins, when his first-class career ended in 1995. He had the potential to be a very great batsman indeed, he was a cavalier born into an age in which it was mainly the footsoldiers who held sway. Wayne was held in the highest regard by his contemporaries, not because he was a run cruncher in the Boycott mould, but because his batting could turn a match on its head and often bring his team an unexpected success. Graham Gooch, England's most capped player and highest run-scorer brings this into focus: 'In the 1980s and early 1990s there were probably six outstanding batsmen who could dominate a match by the power of their stroke play. I count myself among them, together with David Gower, Mike Gatting, Allan Lamb, Ian Botham and Wayne Larkins. He really does fit into that company.'

It is, therefore, surprising and even sad to discover that Wayne was selected for England in only thirteen Test matches and twenty-five one day internationals, most of which came at a stage in his career when he could well have been described as a veteran. The selection of English Test teams has long been a source of concern and amazement to cricket followers in Great Britain and, while the idiocies perpetrated by successive selection committees belong to another book, it is instructive to observe, as an example of their folly, that of the 285 cricketers selected for England since the Second World War, sixty were given no more than one or two matches. It is not surprising that the record of English Test cricket in that period has only rarely been a glorious one.

Wayne's professional career can be seen to have had three defining moments, one to his advantage and the other two not. The first occurred in 1974 when, after five and a half seasons on the Northamptonshire staff, it was almost decided not to retain him. Wayne had been a remarkably high scorer for the Second XI, but success at first team level had eluded him. It was fortunate that wiser minds, particularly that of the County secretary, Ken Turner, and the former captain, Keith Andrew, prevailed at that point and in the following season he began to make his mark. He prospered to such an extent that he was called into the England team in the 1979 Prudential Cup and for the final Test match against India, although injury caused his withdrawal from the latter match. Nevertheless he was selected for the tour to Australia and India in the following winter.

Subsequently he was not so lucky. Despite some sterling performances, he failed to make the England side to tour India and Sri Lanka in the winter of 1981/82. Even accounting for the vagaries of the English selection system of the time, he had every reason to expect to be chosen and, when he was ignored, he unwisely accepted the offer to tour South Africa on what is commonly known as the Breweries Tour (not, incidentally, for the volume of beer consumed but rather on account of those who had sponsored this rebel tour). This was, without doubt, his second defining moment. For three weeks' work in the early part of 1982 he earned some £20,000, but soon afterwards he received a three-year ban from Test cricket at a time when his powers were at their greatest.

Although he was picked for England again once the ban had run its course, but was again forced to withdraw through injury, he soldiered on without international recognition through the 1980s and graced the County Championship and the many one-day encounters, until he was finally recalled in 1989, at Graham Gooch's behest and at the age of thirty-six, to play for England in the Nehru Cup in India and to tour the West Indies in the following spring. He failed to gain recognition in the summer of 1990 largely as a result of injury, but secured a tour place to Australia and New Zealand in the winter of 1990/91.

After one further season with Northamptonshire in 1991 he accepted the offer of his former captain and opening partner, Geoff Cook, who was then the director of cricket in the fledgling county of Durham, to join county cricket's eighteenth and latest team. He saw the move as a way of lengthening his career and performed with distinction in his new environment, but at the end of 1995 season, when a benefit with his new county was in the offing, the third defining moment came about. Quite unexpectedly and, to most dispassionate observers, quite unjustly, his contract was not renewed. At the age of forty-two he found himself in the cricketers' departure lounge, facing an uncertain future. We must be glad that he has shown a bold face to adversity, displaying all the panache of his best batting and now, playing for Bedfordshire, the county of his youth, he destroys Minor Counties' bowling just as effectively as he once bludgeoned first-class bowlers at the pinnacle of his career.

What follows is, therefore, a story of great under-recognition, of a man seen by England's selectors through a glass darkly. Wayne's life has not been without its personal tribulations. His first marriage ended in divorce, and he is sad that he rarely sees his two daughters. It is true that he tends to enjoy more than just the one pint and that his time-keeping is barely compatible with the Greenwich system, but he has always shown the utmost pride in his chosen profession and has gradually come to terms with his destiny. After his sojourn in the North he is now back in the Midlands with his new family, but life is not easy. One thing that Wayne Larkins definitely lacks is about eighty England Test caps to tell his grandchildren about.

Post Office cover showing Wayne in full flow.

Invitation for Wayne to attend a barbecue while on the Australian tour of 1990.

1

A BEDFORDSHIRE YOUTH

In 1953 everythingwas starting to go well in England after the privations and austerity of the Second World War and the immediate years following it. In May Edmund Hillary and Sherpa Tensing had scaled Everest and in June the country had witnessed the Coronation of the young Queen Elizabeth the Second. For cricket lovers, however, something of perhaps even greater significance had happened: England had wrested the Ashes from Australia.

The Australians, who had held the mystical Ashes since the 1932/33 winter season, were making their second post-war tour. Len Hutton, England's first professional captain, had been confirmed in the post for his second season running, having decisively defeated India in the Tests in the previous summer. The First Test of the five-match series against Australia had ended in a draw, although Alec Bedser had distinguished himself with seven wickets in the first innings, but it had been insufficient to defeat the Australians, while the Second Test had also seen no positive result, despite Len Hutton's magnificent 145 in the first innings and the famous match-saving partnership between Willie Watson and Trevor Bailey that had ensured a draw. The third and fourth matches had gone the same way, although England had escaped defeat at Leeds only by the use of some distinctly dubious bowling by Bailey, who bowled consistently down the leg-side with no slip, conceding a mere 9 runs from 6 overs, as the Australians sought to reach their winning target. Nowadays the match referee might have shown more than a passing interest. The sides proceeded, therefore, to the Oval in August with all to play for. England gained a modest first-innings lead, but in Australia's second innings the deadly Surrey combination of right- and left-arm spin served up by Jim Laker and Tony Lock had dismissed Australia for 162. Although Hutton had been run out for 17 and England generally had made heavy weather of the scoring the 132 needed for victory, they had in the end achieved a deserved win when Denis Compton swept the occasional left-arm spin of Arthur Morris to the square leg boundary. The Ashes, held by Australia for twenty years, had returned to England. It confirmed that English cricket, which had started poorly after the Second World War, was coming back to its best again.

This view was reinforced by the winter tour to the West Indies in 1953/54, when England, two down after two Tests, came back to square the series at Sabina Park, Jamaica with a dominating win by nine wickets. Once again, Len Hutton had led England from the front and ended the series with eight innings, producing 677 runs at an average in excess of 96. Such achievements seem almost incredible in the media-exposed world of today's cricket, but this was perhaps a more heroic age.

Life was also going along very well in 1953 in the village of Roxton, a quiet spot not far from the A1 and close to Bedford. Here Jack and Mavis Larkins celebrated the birth of their second son, Wayne, on 22 November. The couple both hailed from this flat, but green and leafy, part of agricultural Bedfordshire. Jack had been born in 1918 and came from the village of Staploe near St Neots. In 1939 he had met Mavis Jefferies, of similar age and one of four sisters who lived in Roxton, and they had married in 1942 while Jack was on leave from the Royal Navy. He had served with some distinction on minesweepers during the Second World War, had been badly wounded by shrapnel off Gibraltar while serving with the Mediterranean Fleet and had come home with a chestful of medals. Just after the war their first son, Melvin, was born and Jack returned to civilian life working on the land around Roxton and doing some light building work. When she was not looking after the family, Mavis helped out on some farms at harvest time.

Roxton itself is a compact little village with some three to four hundred inhabitants and it boasts, besides the parish church of St Mary Magdalen, a quite unusual Congregational Church, created in 1808 from a barn with a thatched roof. Its High Street, now barely troubled by traffic, was probably once part of the Great North Road, which crossed the Ouse by a ford between Tempsford and Roxton. Nowadays the village is sheltered from the busy A428 by the Park, a large green which contains Roxton House, the home of the Metcalf family for three hundred years, and, more importantly, the ground of Roxton Cricket Club. Jack, a sound but not outstanding cricketer, played here. Later he was joined in Roxton teams by the young Melvin, now enjoying the nickname Ned, which he was to pass on to his younger brother. At the age of five Wayne started at the local primary school but, as is the case at many junior schools, very little cricket was played there. Wayne recalls that it was largely 'six over the churchyard wall and out'. Soon he was joining his father and his brother at the Park on Saturday afternoons and, like all younger brothers, he spent a fair amount of time in the scorebox. From time to time, he was even chosen to play.

Today, life in Roxton has doubtless changed from how it was at the end of the 1960s, but at that time it was a close-knit society. As Will Stapleton, the village historian, has said:

Wayne's parents' wedding, 1942.

Roxton Congregational Church, with its thatched roof.

Wayne's parents, Jack and Mavis Larkins.

Wayne, aged eight, with his parents at a relative's wedding.

Roxton Cricket Club ground.

Wayne, aged eleven.

'Help and kindness were out of this world when anyone needed support. No matter what the cause we always pulled together.' Yet he also observed with a degree of irony: 'One had to be careful what one said to a neighbour because so many were related down to second and third cousins.' It was in such a society that Wayne Larkins grew up and one can still see its companionable, even chummy, atmosphere reflected in him today. Christmas festivities, evening and weekend gatherings were spent at the houses of grandmother Jefferies or one of Mavis's three sisters, Phyllis, Kath or Elsie. 'We were a very close family and Christmas parties seemed to go on for a week or more', Wayne recalls. In the holidays they went off with Uncle Gordon and his wife Thelma in a Ford Prefect for caravan holidays at Great Yarmouth.

The Larkins certainly were a cricketing family. Jack thoroughly enjoyed the game and played for Roxton for many years before taking up umpiring in his forties. Melvin developed into a more than useful all-rounder for Bedford Town, while Aunt Phyllis's son, Graham Mallett, made his mark in club cricket and Kath's grandson, Mark Hodgson, a fast bowler and hard-hitting batsman, secured a trial with Northamptonshire.

The Larkins lived in a council house at 9 Ford Lane, and Jack and his two sons played cricket all through the year on the green strip in the centre of the concrete road outside the house, with nothing more than a box as a wicket. Jack bowled for hours on end at his sons and it did not take Wayne long to show a real appetite for the game. 'He played the game as soon as he was big enough to hold a bat', Melvin has commented. Will Stapleton, who lived in the Old Bakehouse soon after he had married, recalls seeing the Larkins' games of cricket and the attendant damage to the windows of Ford Lane. He used to see Wayne practising all alone there for hours on end, throwing the ball up with his left hand and then playing his strokes.

In 1965, at the age of eleven, Wayne left the cosy atmosphere of Roxton's Junior School and headed for Bushmead School, a mixed secondary modern school of some 350 pupils

Wayne, aged fifteen.

Longsands (above) versus Bushmead (Wayne's school). Wayne is in the front row, second from left.

at Eaton Socon, where Jack London and, later, Tom Bishop, held the post of headmaster. Academic work was not high on Wayne's list of priorities, unlike football and cricket. Brian Odell, a newly qualified PE master at Bushmead, noted Wayne's precocious ability in both games and believed that the status and recognition Wayne acquired as a result of his sporting ability satisfied his ego sufficiently for him not to see the need to make academic progress. If things did not come easily to him, he would seem not to really bother, except in matters of sport, where he never missed a game.

By his early teens Wayne was, at five feet nine inches, approaching his full adult height. He was a good deal taller than his peers, so much so that older boys always sought to have him included in their teams. When he was in the second form it was always likely that people wanted him to play for the fourth form team. Brian encouraged him throughout and in the winter season Wayne kept goal for the school soccer teams. In the summer he soon became a star on the cricket field. At one stage Brian believed that he would make an even better footballer than cricketer and was very disappointed when he did not get him selected for the England Under 15 squad.

In those days headmasters were always keen to ensure that sporting achievement brought kudos to their schools. Jack London and Tom Bishop were no exception to this rule and Wayne, seen very much as a man's man, was hugely popular for this reason. Wayne helped Bushmead to become a particularly successful sporting school during his time there, and in 1968 this small secondary modern school won the Huntingdon County Football Cup, defeating many much larger establishments. Fame, however, did not alter his essentially modest and self-effacing character. Schoolmasters the world over often encounter boys of superior sporting ability which leads to them being boastful and disdainful of their comrades. With Wayne the reverse was the case: he remained unassuming, but quietly secure in the knowledge of his ability. It was not only in football and cricket that he excelled. Brian Odell recalls: 'He was an outstanding natural athlete who could throw, jump and run any distance from 100 yards to cross country.' In fact, the Cambridgeshire archives for Bushmead School still record that in 1967 Wayne Larkins won the junior 100 and 220 yards, together with the record for throwing the cricket ball.

It was not only in sport that Wayne showed a precocious interest. Brian Odell relates that he was 'often close to the older girls at school, not because he sought their company, but rather the reverse'. Well past his fortieth birthday, Wayne still retains a clear and vivid recollection of one old flame in particular, the lovely Denise Rowe, whose father kept a shop in Eaton Ford.

In the 1960s David Wilson held the post of county games adviser for Huntingdonshire. He often visited Bushmead and he soon recognised Wayne's enormous talent on the games field and involved him in Huntingdon teams both at cricket and soccer. He recalls that he found it difficult to improve on Wayne's batting technique by the time he had reached the age of fourteen or fifteen. 'A beautiful striker of the ball, a kind lad, no side to him whatsoever' is his recollection. Wayne recalls an early match for the Huntingdon junior side when they played against Yorkshire at Orton Longueville School, near Peterborough. The Yorkshiremen had included Peter Booth, soon to make his name as a fast bowler for MCC schools and later for Leicestershire, and his reputation among schoolboys was enormous. Coming from a county with no first-class connections, most of the Huntingdon team had apparently seemed intimidated by the prospect of playing the mighty Yorkshire side, but Wayne was totally unflappable, and he played Booth with ease and scored a fast 54.

In the summer of 1968, probably in anticipation of Wayne's forthcoming fifteenth birthday in November, Jack Larkins gave Wayne his first new bat, a Slazenger 'Colin Cowdrey Autograph' and not long afterwards it was put to good use. Jack London had left Bushmead and taken over the headship of a school in Martham near Great Yarmouth in Norfolk and it was decided to offer Bushmead a match against the headmaster's new school. It was a long trip for a boys' game of cricket, but Wayne put it to good advantage, scoring 131 out of his school's 164. Martham were no match for this and were out for 99.

When his playing days were over and having umpired for Roxton for a few years, Jack Larkins offered his services to Bedford Town when Melvin started to play there. The whole family often made it the centre of their weekend activities with Jack umpiring, Melvin playing for the Second XI and Wayne and his mother spectating. In 1968, in an early season match versus Dunstable, the team found itself short of a player and Wayne, still aged only fourteen, was drafted in to play. He surprised even his own family by scoring a rapid 58, and after that he was regularly considered for selection. One Sunday the family travelled down to London for a match against Winchmore Hill. Mike Green, now a stalwart of Bedfordshire's committee, was playing in the match and recalls a famous victory. Bedford Town's opponents had rattled up a good 180, and after tea had reduced Bedford to about 60 for five wickets. Wayne came in at number seven to join Mike, who saw little prospect of a win. 'Play yourself in and get some batting practice as we seem as if we are not going to win this one', he advised Wayne. The fourteen-year-old was having nothing of this defeatist talk and tore into the Winchmore Hill bowling to such an extent that the 180 was reached without the loss of another wicket. Mike Green defended stoutly for 30 not out and Wayne walked off the field with an undefeated 74, which included several sixes into the tennis courts at square leg. 'Is that all right then, Mr Green?' he asked perkily as they got back to the pavilion. At the end of this season Wayne had scored 450 runs at an average of over 26. It was no wonder that he found himself mentioned in the club's Annual Report: 'In Wayne Larkins the club has a tremendous prospect, as his feat of topping the batting averages of the Sunday Second XI and the 'Ramblers' testifies.'

Wayne's life at this time was really one long round of sport. Apart from playing school soccer, he spent most winter weekends playing for the Great Barford Youth Club Team and even managed to get a trial for Tottenham Hotspur, no longer as a goalkeeper, but as a centre forward. 'I want to be a professional footballer and cricketer', he explained at the time. 'I shall be leaving school soon after Easter 1969, and I'd like to play soccer for Spurs and cricket for Hampshire.' In fact, Spurs turned him down for an apprenticeship at that point, but were sufficiently interested to come back to Eaton Socon Football Club and St Neots Town, where Wayne did his training, to see him in the following year. The desire to play for Hampshire was perhaps surprising, but really just boyish enthusiasm. In May 1968 Wayne had gone to see Bedfordshire play Hampshire at Goldington in the second round of the Gillette Cup. The visitors amassed a huge 321 for four wickets in their 60 overs with Roy Marshall, the former West Indian Test batsman, and Barry Reed both scoring centuries. Bedfordshire's reply was a modest 197. When Wayne saw the poor performance of a number of the Bedford Town First XI players, whom he had previously

South Hunts Junior Football XI. Wayne is in the back row as goalkeeper, fourth right.

Wayne, aged fifteen, as best man at his brother Melvin's wedding, at St Neots church in 1968.

admired from his own position in the second team, he was overcome by an urge to be involved in Hampshire cricket, 'to be part of the real action', as he recalls many years later. His yearning for Hampshire cricket was, however, to remain unfulfilled, because Dennis Brookes, the Northamptonshire County Coach, on advice from David Wilson, had taken note of him. 'We put him into the nets', Dennis recalls, 'but frankly we just could not get him out.'

A sudden and tragic event befell the Larkins family in the autumn of 1968. Jack had returned home one evening from working in the fields and announced to Mavis that he had a problem moving his right leg. At first it was not thought to be anything serious by the family doctor, but Mavis, with great determination, ensured that he was examined at Bedford Hospital and the diagnosis, sadly, was cancer. As so often happens in life, a whole host of events coincided. Melvin had been engaged to Diane for a year and in early December they married at St Neots Church. Wayne, barely past his fifteenth birthday, was his brother's best man and Jack, thought to be in remission, but accompanied by a nurse and in a wheelchair, was brought from Bedford to join in the happy occasion. The remission was not to last for long. On Christmas Day 1968, Jack Larkins died in Bedford Hospital. He was only fifty. 'He dealt in a sensible way with the early death of his father,' Brian Odell recalls, 'and this sad event may have matured him.'

Mavis suddenly found herself totally responsible for a fifteen-year-old boy who was mad about sport, but who had few other qualifications. David Wilson had been talking at this time to Tom Bishop, who had now succeeded Brian London as headmaster at Bushmead, and it was agreed that they would again be in touch with Dennis Brookes at Northampton. Wayne's final report from his form master, Mr David Rudd, at Bushmead read:

> Wayne is an outstanding sportsman, but he seriously lacks stamina for other school activities. He has the ability to be a good all-rounder, but so far he has only allowed one part of himself to develop properly. A bit more energy on other activities would pay off handsomely.

During the early summer of 1969, Wayne continued to play for Bedford Town and, not surprisingly after his performances in the seconds, found himself in the First XI. Aged only fifteen and playing on an adult team, he scored handsomely, but it was undoubtedly with great relief that Mavis received a letter in May 1969, from Ken Turner, the secretary of Northamptonshire County Cricket Club, to say that he had interviewed Wayne and that he would be taken on the staff for the months of June, July and August and be paid £7 per week. 'It is hoped', he concluded, 'that he will show sufficient promise to be regarded as a potential first-class cricketer.'

Wantage Road, the home of Northamptonshire County Cricket, beckoned. A great opportunity for Wayne to do what he did best had suddenly presented itself. It became the centre of his professional life for over twenty years.

2

SLOW OFF THE MARK

When Wayne Larkins arrived at Wantage Road, Northampton, the headquarters of the County Cricket Club, he was joining a county that, by the standards of the great teams from Yorkshire, Lancashire and the Home Counties, might have been seen by some people as unfashionable. Although a cricket club had been in existence in Northampton from about 1820, it was not until 1905 that the County joined the ranks of the first-class clubs. Only Glamorgan in 1921 and Durham in 1992 have shorter pedigrees. Northamptonshire was, in fact, for much of its early history a Cinderella among the counties in the Championship. In the seventeen seasons between 1923 and 1939 the County was bottom of the Championship in eight seasons and second to bottom in a further five. The year 1925 was a highlight when it climbed to the dizzy heights of eleventh place.

Things did not look particularly bright after the Second World War either and only Sussex kept Northamptonshire off the bottom in 1946, after which they sank back to their almost habitual place for the next two seasons. The acquisition of Raman Subba Row from Surrey in the mid-1950s had made a significant difference to the batting. Progress, however, began to be made and, after an excellent second place in 1957 under the leadership of Dennis Brookes, nowadays the grand old man of Northamptonshire cricket, the County reached the 1960s in sound, although by no means scintillating, shape. Raman Subba Row had become captain in 1958, but when he retired from cricket in 1962 he was replaced as captain by Keith ('KV') Andrew, 'still regarded by many shrewd judges as the best wicketkeeper in the country,' as the *Playfair Annual* described him at the time. He can be numbered amongst the Northamptonshire players not to have been given their proper due by the England selectors. In the 1954/55 tour of Australia, when Len Hutton's team, spearheaded by Brian Statham and Frank Tyson, routed the Australian batsman, he had been an understudy to the legendary Godfrey Evans and had made one single Test appearance, while in 1963 he was recalled, strangely perhaps given his age of thirty-four, for one Test against the West Indians. In general, however, despite having been recognised for many years in the second half of the 1950s and the early 1960s as England's premier 'keeper he had been sidelined by the selectors' desire to strengthen England's batting by playing high-scoring wicketkeeper batsmen such as Jim Parks and John Murray. One is bewildered by the selectors' willingness to flout the old adage that you always pick your best wicketkeeper even if he cannot bat.

Keith Andrew had inherited a team in 1962 with very few Northamptonshire-born players; in fact, the term 'league of nations' was sometimes used in this context. Quite a number of the 'foreigners' had been recruited from the North East by Doug Ferguson, himself a native of that part of the country and an occasional Second XI player for Northamptonshire. Hailed nowadays by Keith Andrew as 'one of the unsung coaches of English cricket', Doug had found a string of players who would play a vital part in Northamptonshire cricket for that decade and beyond. Malcolm Scott had made his debut in 1959 and he was followed in 1960 by Colin 'Ollie' Milburn, in 1966 by Peter Willey, and two years later by George Sharp. Keith Andrew welded his side together and, according to Mike Brearley, 'his captaincy approach, dealing with a relatively poor county side, was to try to give his team the experience of *not* losing – which often meant playing for a draw.' Eventually he did much better than that and, in 1965, the County Championship title was within their grasp. In August they were twenty-eight points clear and the Committee at Wantage Road had begun to deliberate how they might best celebrate their success, but, sadly, they lost badly to Worcestershire and failed to beat Gloucestershire, while the Worcestershire side wrapped up their remaining fixtures and pipped Northamptonshire at the post by four points. Another season went by and Keith Andrew retired, to be replaced in 1967 by Roger Prideaux.

When Wayne left 9 Ford Lane in Roxton in June 1969 and caught the 128 United Counties bus along the A428 to Northampton, he was still not yet sixteen years old. He found that the County Cricket Club had arranged digs for him with Mrs Baker at 9 Abington Grove. At weekends he went home to Roxton and played cricket for Bedford Town First XI, which had a fine fixture list, including some prominent London clubs. This was all very different from the sleepiness of Roxton and the cosy environment of the Bushmead School. One difference was clear from the start: he had been a star at Bushmead and in the Huntingdonshire Schools team and quite often with Bedford Town and had never needed to push himself to achieve sporting success. Now he was a lad from a rural background who had come to a first-class county club where Roger Prideaux, capped three times by England, was captain. Only a short time before he had been imagining himself in the role of Roger or other Northamptonshire notables and now he was actually their colleague!

Playing alongside him in the team were figures such as Mushtaq Mohammad, who had begun his first-class career at the age of thirteen and played for Pakistan when he was fifteen, Peter Willey, a prodigy who had made his first-class debut when only sixteen and a half, David Steele, Brian Crump and a whole host of other experienced cricketers. Colin Milburn was also a leading figure at the start of the 1969 season, but a significant misfortune befell the club in May, when he was injured in a car accident when returning home after a party to celebrate the defeat of the West Indian touring team at Wantage Road. He lost an eye and the vision in his other eye was seriously impaired. The County, as well as England, had lost a highly talented and aggressive opener. It is perhaps ironic that, later in the 1970s, the England selectors never really grasped the fact that Wayne Larkins had the potential to take over Colin's role.

At that time the pressures on young players were certainly not as great as they are today – indeed, it was probably a good time to be involved in cricket. Geoff Cook observes: 'There seemed to many to be almost endless chances for contracts and, if a player did reasonably well, a certain faith was placed in him.' How starkly that contrasts with today's situation where a young player must produce the goods at an early stage, show that he has the right credentials and then hope that the financial restraints of the county club will allow him to be employed in the following season.

For Wayne, life was very different and perhaps a little daunting, but the digs with Mrs Baker were fine and he was earning his own money, a modest £7 per week for the months of June, July and August. Alan Hodgson was certainly pleased to see Wayne join the County Staff because he was now no longer the youngest professional and Wayne had to take on the role of doing errands for the senior players. 'Things like nipping down to the shops for a packet of fags for the capped men was always the task of the latest arrival', Alan recalls. On other occasions the youngsters really did find themselves literally doing the dirty jobs. In what proved to be Colin Milburn's last Sunday League match, the score-book shows that he 'retired ill.' In fact he had drunk somewhat unwisely on the Saturday night and, having scored five runs, he ran a short single and promptly vomited on the pitch. The youngest professional, armed with a bag of sawdust, found that he had a job to do! However, it was an essentially marvellous time with the teams practising in the County Ground nets under the watchful eye of Dennis Brookes and Percy Davis. There were some strict rules: young pros turned up fully changed at ten o'clock in the morning and practised in the nets in the morning and afternoon unless there was some form of match. If they were lucky they might get Friday afternoons off when Dennis Brookes took his place on the Justices' Bench. There were, of course, some mid-week matches for the Second XI where Wayne acquitted himself tolerably well for a fifteen-year-old, playing 13 innings for 119 runs, with a top score of 30 not out and an average of 11.90. He found another young player already there who also happened to be called Wayne. This was Wayne Osman, a left-handed batsman from Hertfordshire, who was three years older than Wayne Larkins and had been on the Lord's Ground Staff. They enjoyed a certain rivalry.

When the autumn came and the cricket season had closed, Wayne had no choice but to return to Roxton. He was approaching his sixteenth birthday, but he had no qualifications other than his potentially great sporting ability. Apart from cricketing experience at Northampton, the only thing that he had acquired since leaving school was his brother's nickname, Ned. It has remained with him throughout his life, even in the domestic situation.

He found a job working as a brickie's labourer on a housing estate in Eaton Socon and he cannot pass it even today without some recollections of working there. 'Not all my memories of that time were good ones,' he recalls, thinking most certainly of the unremitting frosty

Wayne, aged seventeen, in his early years at Northampton County Cricket Club.

mornings. Later on he worked for the Goodwin Tarmac Company in Great Barford. Mike Goodwin had been his best friend at Bushmead and found him a job in his father's company. Yet it was not all work and no play. Having exchanged the position of goalkeeper for that of centre forward, which was certainly more in line with his image of himself, Wayne was able to join up with his soccer friends at Great Barford Youth Club and play for Eaton Socon, perhaps keeping alive the thought that professional soccer might be the other half of his life.

For Wayne the next two cricket seasons of 1970 and 1971 did not differ greatly from his first experience of professional cricket in the summer of 1969. He continued to practise hard and play cricket whenever and wherever he could and he enjoyed another sound, but not spectacular, season with the Second XI and for other clubs in Northampton, when the County did not require his services. Sadly, he fell way behind his namesake, Wayne Osman, who scored over 1,500 runs in the two seasons for the Second XI, while he himself could manage fewer than 900, although he did pass 50 on one occasion. In the second half of the 1970 season two further tyros had been sent down to Northampton from the North East by Doug Ferguson. Geoff Cook came from Middlesbrough, and was to become Northamptonshire's longest serving captain and, sadly for both men, Wayne's nemesis at Durham, while Alan Tait was from Washington and at the time was regarded by the *cognoscenti,* such as Ken Turner, as the best of the bunch of new players. They added much competition to the two young pros in situ and, at the start of the 1971 season, all four were vying for places. Geoff and Alan must have seemed to the two Waynes like intruders moving into their patch, but it is clear that they managed to tolerate one another reasonably well. Yet, as Geoff Cook recalls, 'in a professional set-up, almost by definition, you try to create a life for yourself and dedicate as much time and effort as possible to furthering your own career.'

The young professionals played a number of two-day Second XI matches and some social cricket for a local club, the Saints, in Northampton. 'We were lucky, ' Geoff remembers,' to be under that patient and totally unhistrionic coach, Dennis Brookes. There can seldom have been better coaches on the art of batting.' On non-match days the strict regime of practice continued at Wantage Road. Three hours in the morning were followed by a short break for lunch and then a further two hours in the nets, all of which was rounded off by fielding competitions. Wayne was clearly as enthusiastic as any of them and in terms of fielding, probably the most proficient because of his great natural physical ability.

Other young pros like Ian Watson and Chris Stone also appeared on the scene and the former proved a very heavy scorer notching over 850 runs for the Second XI in the 1971 season. Geoff Cook, who was doubtless more thoughtful and thus more mature than some of the other young pros, was offered a chance of First XI cricket two-thirds of the way through his first season. He seized the opportunity with both hands and notched up over 600 runs by September, including an undefeated 122 against Sussex. It seemed as if Wayne was going to be left behind. 'This certainly created some distance between Wayne on the one hand and Alan Tait and me on the other' says Geoff Cook. At the end of the season, however, Dennis Brookes retained Wayne, together with Alan and Geoff, while the others were handed their cards. Ian Watson who, in Geoff Cook's delightful phrase, 'scored millions of runs for the Second XI' headed back to the south and Wayne Osman, despite some real success, returned to Hertfordshire to become a policeman.

The 1972 season started, therefore, with Wayne well behind the competition. Geoff Cook and Alan Tait found themselves opening the Northamptonshire innings together until well into July and both of them finished the season with impressive figures, scoring over 750 and 550 runs respectively. Wayne did not enjoy such an auspicious beginning and, by comparison with his young colleagues, his performance was pretty much a complete disaster. In five matches and batting in eight innings, he was able to compile a mere 35 Championship runs at an average of five with a top score of 20 against Gloucestershire, and in five Sunday League games he did little better. On the credit side, however, his performances in the Second XI brought him the team's highest run total for the season. He was beginning to show something that may perhaps have dogged him throughout his career – the inability to adapt quickly to a new environment. 'This reflected his personality as much perhaps as his cricketing ability', is a view expressed by Geoff Cook. The winters were, in some senses, a consolation. Having now moved to Northampton on a permanent basis, he was able to find work finishing the welts of shoes in a randing firm on the Moulton Park Industrial Estate, where he worked alongside Alan Tait. Better still, he was also getting some games of soccer as a semi-professional with Wolverton.

The early 1970s were really quite promising years for a young player to make his mark in Northamptonshire, because the County was going through a period of reconstruction. At the end of the 1970 season Roger Prideaux resigned the captaincy and left the county ostensibly for 'business reasons', although this did not prevent him from turning out in twenty-two matches for Sussex in the following season. The rest reads a little like a catalogue: Brian Reynolds retired after twenty years' service in 1970, Hylton Ackerman returned to South Africa after the 1971 season, while Peter Lee, one of the very few players who was actually from Northamptonshire, went up to Old Trafford at the same time. Brian Crump, who had been on the staff for twelve years, called it a day at the end of the 1972 season. Dennis Breakwell went south to try his chances with Somerset in 1973, while Sarfraz Nawaz, the Pakistani opening bowler, was put out to grass for a couple of seasons. Colin Milburn never recovered properly from his serious injuries and had to give up the game. This was perhaps one drinking partner fewer for Wayne, although he doubtless found a number more.

It was, however, not all loss. On the plus side can be counted the fact that Jim Watts was appointed captain for the 1971 season and stayed in the post until the end of the 1974 season, when he left to train as a teacher. He became a decisive influence on Wayne's development and recalls a revealing incident: 'We were playing Glamorgan at Swansea in August 1972, and Wayne was being given a run in the first team. I had won the toss and decided to bat and the openers Geoff Cook and Peter Willey got us off to a good start and David Steele and Mushtaq continued the good work. I had put Wayne in at number five in the hope that there might be some relatively easy runs, but it was not to be. Wayne came in at the fall of David's wicket and was soon lbw to the off-spin of Roger Davis for just 2. I was next in myself and, as I crossed with him on my way to the middle, I noticed that he was crying.' Wayne, perhaps showing the beginning of the pride that he always sought to show in his role as a cricketer, desperately wanted to succeed, but at this stage everything seemed to be conspiring against him. Nowadays Wayne sees Jim Watts as a formative influence on his life. 'He told me to show more backbone and made me face up to things', because, after the incident at Swansea, they chatted and Jim made it wholly clear that there was no future in Wayne's approach. Nowadays a headmaster running his own private school, Jim Watts is a kindly man, but he adds 'Wayne was one of the most natural players I have ever seen, but he always had such an apologetic manner. I suspect he has always underestimated himself through his life.'

Although the County came a disappointing fourteenth in the 1971 season, Jim's leadership, the continued presence of Mushtaq Mohammad and the acquisition of the great Indian slow left-arm bowler, Bishen Bedi, brought them two third places and a fourth place in the County Championship in the next three seasons. Their performance in the one-dayers, by contrast, was far less good: early exits from the Gillette and Benson & Hedges competitions in all four seasons were allied to low positions in the John Player Sunday League in every season except 1974, when a fourth place was some compensation.

It was usual for the young professionals, once the activities of the day had ended, to head off to the local to drink a fair number of pints. Although these young men doubtless enjoyed their cricket, their life had a certain sameness about it and was not at all mentally inspiring. On one occasion in 1972 there was a dinner-cum-party at Tarry's Public House in Harpole not far from Northampton after a charity match in aid of Brian Crump's benefit. Wayne had by this time acquired a sky-blue Ford Anglia with a gold top and, still with a provisional licence, he ferried Geoff Cook, Alan Tait and Norman Maltby, another young professional from Marske in Yorkshire, to Harpole. Unfortunately they had all imbibed too liberally and, on the way home at about 1.00 a.m., they swerved close to a lorry in Gold Street, Northampton, and the driver reported the matter to the police. 'Slam' Eales, their landlord at 42 East Park Parade, where they all now lived, suggested a plea of spiked drinks. 'Slam', one imagines, had perhaps practised his law mainly in the barrack room, and this subterfuge did not hold up in court, particularly as one team-member announced to the court: 'We often do this!' Wayne was fined £35 plus costs and had to garage his Ford Anglia for the next six months. The Chairman of the Bench, Mrs Tasker, was 'quite appalled at the conduct of the members of an otherwise successful county cricket team.' If records were what Wayne was seeking at this time he had certainly scored a winner here. Mavis Larkins was not amused.

There was some compensation for Wayne. In the winter of 1972/73 he had started to play soccer on Saturdays for the East Park Club and on Sundays for the Anglo-Celtic Club, both in Northampton. The manager of the latter club, Mick Edmonds, had some contacts with the League club of Notts County and arranged a trial for Wayne. He played twice for the Notts County reserves in the Football Combination. There was a 0-0 draw with Lincoln City and another draw, this time 1-1, with Rotherham United in which Wayne scored from the centre forward position. However, the manager of Notts County, Jimmy Sewell, sought total dedication from his young professionals and would not countenance their playing two sports, so this opportunity went begging. There can be little doubt that Wayne Larkins possessed outstanding football ability and one may speculate on what course his career might have taken if he had fallen in with Jimmy Sewell and forsaken the game of cricket.

The season of 1973 was a barren and unproductive time for Wayne. There was going to be no breakthrough into the big time. In early May he was picked for the County team, captained by David Steele and containing a few younger players, to play Cambridge University at Fenners. He scored a blistering and exhilarating 109, but this was a false dawn and in the rest of the season he made only another 96 first-class runs in fifteen innings. For the Second XI his performance was acceptable, but by no means outstanding and he managed a few runs on Sundays and in the Benson & Hedges Cup. The winter continued in much the same manner. Randing shoes gave way to sealing beer barrels as a gas-distiller at the Greene King Brewery in Biggleswade, while soccer gave him a small income at Wolverton and, later on, at Wellingborough.

Northamptonshire's secretary was Ken Turner. He came to the County in 1949 as assistant secretary and succeeded the famous Colonel A. St.G. Coldwell in 1958. For twenty-seven years until his retirement in 1985 he had been a force to be reckoned with. 'He was one of the major influences', according to Matthew Engel and Andrew Radd in their history of the

County Club, 'in transforming Northamptonshire from a team which was easy meat for the larger counties in the late 1940s into one of the better sides in the County Championship ... he was the iron foot in the kid boots which kicked the 'Cobblers' upstairs into the trophy winning league'. He also had a decisive effect upon Wayne. At the start of the 1970s the County's finances were not all that they should have been and Ken Turner decided to put the indoor school to good use when cricketers were not using it. He decided he would run evening discos and, although the local police cautioned care, he went ahead with the project, often hoping that the wind would be blowing in the right direction on disco nights to carry the din away from the residential areas and over into Abington Park. One evening in 1973 Wayne, who along with many of the other young pros was a regular at the discos, met Jane Faulkner, a secretary at Shoosmith and Harrison, an old established firm of Northampton solicitors. This was more than a brief meeting. Jane and Wayne spent much free time together and for Wayne it was his first serious romance and something very different from his life of cricket and refreshment with his friends from the Club after the match. When she was not at work, Jane used to come to Wantage Road to watch the cricket and at the end of the season they went on holiday together to the South Coast.

A year later, Wayne had another good reason to be thankful to Ken Turner. He found himself summoned one morning to the formidable secretary's office where the incumbent, sitting laconically, as was his habit, with his feet on the desk, started to berate him about his attitude and his performances. 'I took it on the chin to start with,' Wayne recalls, 'but after a time I answered back and not in the best of language either.' Having rushed out of the secretary's office in an emotional state and without permission, he expected to be called back and handed his P45. Strangely enough, things did not occur quite in the way he had anticipated. On the following morning he found himself back in with Ken Turner, who said: 'That's what I have been wanting to hear from you all along. I would like a much more positive approach from you, my lad, and perhaps a bit more aggression.' An odd method of man-management, perhaps, but it seemed to work. When Wayne's future was in doubt in September 1974, Ken Turner's was one of two voices that saved him from the chop. The domineering bully, as he was perceived by the young pros, actually had a heart of gold.

Wayne was approaching make or break time. At the start of the 1974 season he was starting his sixth summer with the club. He had made just the one hundred against Cambridge University and not much besides. A few runs in the one-day competition scarcely counted in this context. It was really a pretty bleak scenario for a young man who wanted to make a career in first-class cricket and had few qualifications to do otherwise, particularly as he had become engaged to be married to Jane in the early part of the year. He had even debated his future with Alan Hodgson, a fast bowler who had joined the staff a little before him and with whom he had shared digs. He was wondering whether there were perhaps opportunities for young cricketers in the Lancashire leagues.

For the 1974 season the County had registered the outstanding opening batsman Roy Virgin from Somerset and Sarfraz Nawaz had been called back to bolster the bowling. Wayne started the season, unsurprisingly, in the Second XI, but at the beginning of June he was given an extended trial in the First XI and played through that month and into July. In seven Championship matches in which he was batting mainly at number seven, he played 10 innings, scored 54 runs at an average of just over 7 with a top score of 15. He was, of course, sent back smartly to the Second XI. Here he had managed to find his level and ended the season with nearly 1,000 runs at an average of over 40 and with a top score of 137. But a batsman cannot stay in Second XIs forever. When the reckoning came to be made at the end

Northampton County Cricket Club, 1974. From left to right, back row: Geoff Cook, Wayne Larkins, George Sharp, Alan Hodgson, Ray Bailey, Colin Milburn, Alan Tait. Front row: David Steele, Mushtaq Mohammad, Jim Watts (captain), Bob Cottam, John Dye. (Bill Smith)

of the season Wayne, since his first-class debut in 1972, had played 37 innings for the County, scored 312 runs at an average of 9.75 and his ton against Cambridge University in 1973 had been his only worthwhile knock. He had scored a few runs on Sundays, but certainly nothing that would really impress the Committee. Most fair-minded people would have seen Wayne as having had a reasonable trial. He was coming up for his twenty-first birthday and was no longer a beginner. The sack seemed imminent.

The Northamptonshire Committee clearly felt that they had given Wayne every chance, but he was consistently failing to trouble the scorers to any great extent. There comes a point when 'promise' is just a word and not a sound investment. Several committee members were inclined to release him, but help was on hand. 'Ken Turner certainly put in a good word for me at that time', Wayne recalls, 'although after that disastrous interview with him I never thought that he would support me after my poor showing.' There was another voice too, one that Wayne never really knew about until many years after, and that was Keith Andrew. The former skipper had become a committee member after he had given up playing and he recalls that, when it was mooted that Wayne was to go, he told the committee – and this was uncharacteristic for such a balanced and thoughtful person –'If Wayne Larkins goes, I shall be going too.' Had the sacking gone ahead there is absolutely no doubt that Keith would have sought another post in cricket and Wayne would have accompanied him.

So Wayne stayed. It had been a close-run thing. The coming season of 1975 was going to be Wayne's last chance.

3
COUNTY CAP

It was perhaps inevitable that Wayne would attract the name of 'Ned'. People by the name of Larkins do, as Melvin, Wayne's elder brother, had found out in his time, but David Steele claims to be the one to have christened Wayne at some stage after his arrival at Wantage Road. It started to stick, although some of the Northants fraternity sometimes prefer 'Larky'.

Jim Watts was Wayne's first county captain and he always kept an eye on him when he started to get some first team cricket because he understood that there was a real talent to be developed, 'He was a lovely lad and a supreme athlete', Jim recalls nowadays. When April nets came along at the County Ground, Wayne would strike the ball with real ease, even though he hadn't practised all winter. Jim recognised in him a style that he now likens to that of Greg Chappell or Martin Crowe, but he also saw seeds of weakness, especially in his social life. 'The young pros at Northants, of course, all enjoyed the drinking life and, while I agree that Wayne was 100 per cent ready to play on the following morning, his frolicking at the bar at the Wantage Road pavilion and other pubs, such as the Coach House Hotel or the Abington, always gave me some cause for concern.' Jim also saw that this lad, so quiet in the dressing room and seeking to take pride in his potential ability, often fretted while waiting to bat. He asked Wayne one day whether he might not feel happier opening the innings. Wayne's response was typical; 'What if I fail?' he lamented.

The same theme appears in the shrewd comments of Alan Hodgson, one of a number of players who came from Durham and who arrived at Northampton in 1968. He became one of Wayne's earliest friends at Northampton and was another tenant at the 'Slam' Eales establishment at 42 East Park Parade. 'Larky dreadfully needed to feel he was one of the team and part of the Club furniture. I certainly agree with the view that Bob Willis has expressed in one of his books, that Larky had little ability to make things happen for himself and tended to take life as it came. Perhaps part of the trouble lay in the fact that he came from rural Bedfordshire, while many of the other younger pros like me who came from the North were obviously much more streetwise.'

The 1975 season, clearly a last chance occasion for Wayne, was about to begin but prior to that a happy occasion on the domestic front took place. On 22 March the twenty-one-year-old Wayne and Jane Faulkner, one year older, were married at the Parish Church in Duston on the outskirts of Northampton. Melvin returned the honours and acted as best man. There was a reception in the church hall, but there was not time for a honeymoon and they moved to a flat in Castle Avenue in Duston to begin their married life.

If this was clearly going to be Wayne's make or break season it was certainly not all plain sailing to start with. Although he was not included in first match at the end of April against Cambridge University where he might have expected a stack of easy runs, he found himself picked for two county matches against Somerset and Warwickshire. He managed, batting at number six, to pick up three successive ducks with a pair against the Midland county. He performed a little better when he was asked, significantly perhaps, to open the innings against Leicestershire and he reached 34 in the second innings. Two more ducks against Glamorgan and Worcestershire sent him catapulted back down to the seconds by the middle of June. He had played nine innings and in five of them he had been out for nought. It was perhaps surprising that no one of the establishment at Northampton CCC, except for Jim Watts, had noticed that Wayne did much better when opening the innings. 'I was struggling badly,' Wayne mused some time after. 'Things were getting dire and I just could not seem to hit the ball in the middle of the bat, although I was doing pretty well in the seconds.' He certainly was! He ended his 1975 Second XI season with nearly 1,000 runs at an average of just under 50.

Wayne, however, was missing out on the real action throughout the rest of June and all of July, when the County was having some mixed results. There were a number of problems in the club which boiled down in essence to one factor: leadership. In the course of 1974 Jim Watts had said that it would be his last season with the county and that he would start training as a teacher, so the captaincy was offered to David Steele, who turned it down on the grounds that 1975 was going to be his benefit year. It also turned out to be the year of his totally unexpected selection for the England Test team and his elevation to national folk-hero. ('The Bank Clerk Goes To War', was Clive Taylor's headline in *The Sun*). Leaving the Lord's home team dressing-room to go out for his first innings for England, David was so unsure of the geography of the pavilion that he ended up in the members' loo on the lower ground floor before he found his way on to the pitch. In spite of these nerves, he tamed the menace of Lillee and Thomson with four half-centuries in three Test matches against Australia.

The choice for the captaincy in 1975 fell, therefore, upon Roy Virgin, who had joined the county from Somerset in 1973 and in the following season notched up over 1,800 runs with seven tons. At the end of July, when the County were well beaten by Middlesex, this amiable man found the pressure too much, with his personal form in tatters, and he resigned the captaincy. Wayne's old mentor, Jim Watts, was recalled from his college vacation, only to have his finger broken in the County's next game against the Australians. David Steele was given a go in a Sunday League match, but when this ploy apparently failed, Mushtaq Mohammad became the fourth Northants captain that season.

This was, in many respects, a stroke of luck for Wayne. Mushtaq had always had a soft spot for Wayne ever since the time when he joined the Northants staff in 1969. 'He was the most talented young player I saw in the English game in the early Seventies,' Mushtaq observed later. 'The trouble was that he enjoyed his pint rather too well and, although I advised him against this, he paid scant attention. For all that, he had the potential to be a great batsman, a marvellous timer of the ball and the best cover fielder in the English game. David Steele once said to me that he would have been happy with half of Wayne's talent. I think it is fair to say that he learned quite a lot about cricket from me. Of course, had he been a Pakistani he would have got into Test cricket very much earlier than he did, probably in about 1976. The trouble with English cricket is that the counties keep these lads for too long in the second teams while older pros of lesser ability hang around for a benefit season and the Test selectors never seem to take a chance, particularly with players from less fashionable counties such as Leicester, Derby and Northants.'

Some feel that Jim Watts was possibly too much of a schoolmaster for Wayne, who was often in awe of him. Mushtaq's appointment as captain was like 'taking the cork out of the bottle for Ned', as David Steele explained it. It was not surprising, therefore, that Wayne found himself called back to the County team in August. Earlier in the season Fred Swarbrook's slow left-arm had cleaned him up in the Derby match and, when he was recalled to the first team against Hampshire at Bournemouth, he was once again undone by two slow left-armers, John Southern and Peter Sainsbury.

For the next match Northants moved up to Chelmsford where, almost predictably it seems, he fell to the left-handed Ray East of Essex in the first innings. An irony if ever there was one: Wayne in his prime was to become the scourge of all slow left-armers on the county circuit! Northants, boosted by 80s from Geoff Cook and Sarfraz Nawaz, had scored 309, to which Essex had replied with 366 for 6 declared. In their second knock Northants had lost their first three wickets for twenty-one runs and were in danger of losing the match when Wayne, batting at number five and with a season's batting average of eight point something, joined Mushtaq. Together they added 273 in five hours, breaking in the process a Northamptonshire record for the fourth wicket which had stood since 1910 as they surged past the 232 scored at Portsmouth by two great names in the County's history, George Thompson and the West Indian S.G. Smith, only five years after the county had entered the County Championship. Such a performance was all in a day's work for Mushtaq, but for Wayne, with his string of inexplicable first team failures behind him, it was something rather more important. 'It was the greatest day of my life, cricket-wise anyway,' he said at the time. A first Championship century is a milestone in any batsman's career. The game, in fact, turned into a complete damp squib, as Essex, still seeking a high place in the table, continued to bowl large numbers of bouncers at Mushtaq and Wayne and so did not induce the former to declare and offer his opponents a total to chase. Many of the bouncers came from Essex's West Indian fast bowler, the late Keith Boyce, who, becoming over-excited, twice had Wayne caught at square leg off no-balls on his lunch-time score of 99. Nowadays Wayne recalls with a gentle smirk from beneath his ample moustache 'He wasn't that happy either'. One more single before lunch might have aided Wayne's digestion powerfully, but for someone whose nerve had been considered suspect, he remained, as one of the *Northampton Chronicle & Echo* reporters noted, 'outrageously cool', ate a hearty steak and kidney pie lunch and then went on to complete his ton and reach 127 before he was caught at long-on by Pont, substituting for Graham Gooch, off an occasional bowler, the South African Kenny McEwen. 'I am sure it was largely a question of confidence', Wayne said at the time. "I needed to get into double figures and, when I had made twenty, I really felt a lot better.'

August was proving to be an outstanding month for Wayne. Just prior to his triumph at Chelmsford he had been the only Northants batsman to put up any form of showing in the Sunday League match against Derbyshire. Although the County went down to their fourth Sunday defeat in a row, Wayne played to his potential. He found himself batting at number five with only 100 on the board after 20 overs and with an even less experienced partner in Richard Williams at the other end. Wayne took charge of the situation scoring 53 in 44 minutes with two clean sixes and five other boundaries. Wayne capped this fateful season with a sparkling 59 out of a partnership with Peter Willey of 86 in 78 minutes in the County's final game against Warwickshire at Edgbaston. It was then back to establishing a home with Jane and working in the British Shoe Corporation in Barry Road, Northampton. Football provided some distraction from the boredom of his winter job.

Wayne, an effective bowler, rarely performed to his potential. (Bob Thomas)

At the start of the 1976 season Wayne found that his previous season's exploits had guaranteed him a place in the first team for most of the season. This was going to be a momentous season for Northants in that they were to win the Gillette Cup and come second in the County Championship. After three matches in April and May, Wayne found himself dropped in favour of Richard Williams for the Yorkshire match at Wantage Road. The affront to his dignity was considerable and, when selected for the Second XI in a match against Nottinghamshire at Horton, he produced such a scintillating all-round performance that he almost won the game on his own. Scoring 101 with 9 fours and 2 sixes in the first innings total of 182 for 8, he then destroyed the Notts' first knock with an analysis of 7 for 31 in only eleven overs. Following this, he scored 103 in Northants' second innings and Notts slunk back to Trent Bridge with their tails between their legs, having lost by 146 runs in a relatively low scoring match. Restored to the first team, Wayne did not look back and played in all the remaining county matches. His bowling, ironically enough, seemed for a week or two to be his main strength. Against the powerful West Indies in their tour match at the county ground he dismissed both their openers, Lawrence Rowe and his very own hero, Gordon Greenidge. The latter had joined Hampshire in 1970 and, six years on, having formed an impressive opening partnership for his county with Barry Richards, the South African, he was a force to be reckoned with in all forms of cricket. Wayne had begun to admire his attacking style of opening the batting and longed to emulate it. Some would say that, in the end, he did just that. Later on, against Somerset, he again bowled well and took three wickets, with *Wisden* referring to the West Country county succumbing to 'the pace of Larkins and Sarfraz' – fame indeed! In this match Peter Willey scored a massive 227 and was run out by Wayne when he refused a quick single. Peter did not forget this when Wayne was scoring his double hundreds in 1983. 'I felt it was the day on which I might have got 300,' Peter lamented later, 'but Larky was back on his heels and did not respond.' Although he got a good fifty in this match he was still not getting a chance at opening the innings, as Geoff Cook and Roy Virgin were well ensconced there, but number six in the batting order soon gave way to number five and by the time of the Warwickshire match in July Wayne was up to number four and scored a massive 167 at Edgbaston with 21 fours and 2 sixes in 280 minutes. This was at the time the highest score by a Northants batsman at Edgbaston and beat the 163 scored by Wayne's batting mentor, Dennis Brookes, which had been set as long ago as 1946. 'I felt really pleased when the scoreboard went past 127,' Wayne said at the time. 'I just can't explain what it feels like to score that amount of runs in a first-class game. I was definitely going for the 200 when I was out.'

In the return match with the Midland county there was a pleasant surprise for Wayne and Alan Hodgson. On the second and final day of the match, which Northants won comfortably by an innings, Mushtaq came over at teatime to the two young pros and told them that they had been awarded their county caps. 'I do not think that either of us expected it, said Alan, 'but Mushtaq just came across at teatime and presented us with our caps.' Wayne added, 'I suppose the team had being doing well and we have both chipped in with some useful performances. We were both really pleased.' In fact, Wayne had just cause to be pleased. Less than two years previously he had nearly gone out of the county game and would have ended up in a Lancashire League side. Wayne and Alan celebrated in style with champagne at the *Dog and Duck* in Wellingborough and he still has the champagne cork from the first bottle they cracked. It was a great evening full of alcohol and the joys of success. It was not, of course, only in status that Wayne had gained now that he had been awarded his county cap. It meant a substantial increase in salary. 'I no longer had to borrow a fiver for a pint and some fags,' he now recalls, 'it was great to be able to treat a few people at the bar.' It also meant that Jane and he were able to move out of their rented flat in Duston and acquire a small 'two-up, two-down' house in Church Street, Moulton, near Northampton.

Their lives were clearly defined by the game of cricket and socialising after the match was always high on the agenda. Audrey Sharp, the wife of George, Northamptonshire's wicketkeeper and now an umpire on both the first-class list and the Test match panel, speaks of the kindness extended to her, when after her wedding she moved down to Northampton. 'Jane and Larky were always so very friendly and kind to me. Having come down from the North East, I felt a little ill at ease in my new surroundings, but that soon passed,' she has recalled later.

The prospect ahead for Wayne was now bright and he showed his pleasure in the Worcester game at Wantage Road. The visitors had scored a useful 313 in their first innings, due largely to an outstanding 166 from the twenty-three-year-old Imran Khan. Fifties from David Steele, Geoff Cook, Roy Virgin and Mushtaq had allowed Northants to reach 395 for seven wickets before declaring with maximum bonus points. In Worcester's second knock New Zealand Test batsman Glenn Turner chipped in with a splendid 120 out of a total of 328. The home county needed 247 to win in two and a quarter hours. Five wickets were down at one time for 131 runs, but Wayne scored 83 with 5 sixes and 6 fours in fifty minutes, putting on 112 in forty minutes for the sixth wicket with Roy Virgin. Northants got home by four wickets with sixteen balls to spare. This innings marked Wayne out as one of the batsmen of his time who could turn a match on its head.

This was clearly something of a needle match as Mushtaq and Norman Gifford, the Worcester captain, were known not to get on well. The wicket was in Wayne's words 'a big turner' and Norman Gifford's left-arm spin, reckoned at the time to be among the best of its kind in the country, landed up in the gardens at square leg on numerous occasions. 'I have always liked left-arm spinners, but I was really not interested in my own total at all. The whole point was to win the game and, thankfully, we did just that', he said at the time. 'They realised then that I could play.' Geoff Cook agreed too: 'It was really the first occasion when his outstanding ability to strike the ball and take a game by the scruff of the neck was seen at first team level.' Wayne's attitude of putting team performance before personal success formed the basis of his cricketing philosophy throughout his career – play hard for the team and forget your own personal score. 'If anyone ever said that Larky was not the very best of team men,' Peter Willey has commented subsequently, 'I would call him a downright liar to his face'. Alan Hodgson also saw this innings as a turning point in Wayne's career. 'If there had been any doubt before about Larky's ability, this innings certainly dispelled it. Folks at Northampton now realised that they had been right to retain him and that there was a massive talent to be exploited.'

The 1976 season, Mushtaq's first full one as skipper, had proved to be momentous for the County. It was Northamptonshire's most successful performance since it became a first-class county in 1905. They won the final of the Gillette Cup – where Wayne, although making little contribution with the bat, bowled 12 tight overs for 31 runs – and, perhaps more significantly, they came second in the County Championship. Mushtaq had recognised at the start of the season that the club possessed players of real ability and his determination to extract the full potential from every one of them ensured that they

Mushtaq leaps over Wayne as they prepare, light-heartedly, for the 1976 Gillette Cup final against Lancashire.

played fine cricket throughout. It was Wayne's good fortune to be part of the County's success at this stage of his career.

Pleased with his new status as a capped player, Wayne now found opportunities opening before him for the winter season. John Dye, the fast left-arm over-the-wicket bowler, who had started his career in Kent but had joined Northants in 1972, had been spending his winters in South Africa and playing for Eastern Province. Knowing that the winter season was always a problem for Wayne, John had arranged the offer of a lucrative contract throughout the off-season to coach students at the University of Salisbury in Rhodesia. A free house, a free car and the equivalent of £60 per week, a very reasonable sum at the time, was an offer not really to be sniffed at. But, sadly, Wayne did just that. 'I was very flattered by the offer and hope that they may consider me again,' he said, but they did not do so, of course. His essential failure to make things work for himself, to trade perhaps on

Wayne celebrates Northamptonshire's win over Lancashire in the 1976 Gillette Cup final at Lord's. (Bob Thomas)

the fact that he was now being described in the press as 'a player of immense talent and potential' was starting to show. Failing to realise that this offer was a sign of his growing reputation in the game, he quoted problems with Jane's chances of re-establishing her job when they returned in the spring and that 'there was just too much to do'. So, laid-back and forsaking Rhodesia's winter sun, Wayne trudged back to his fourth winter in the BSC shoe room at Barry Road, with a little semi-professional soccer at Wellingborough thrown in for good measure.

4
REACHING FOR THE TOP

After their success in the previous season, Northants were looking forward to 1977. Mushtaq was well established in the role of captain and Wayne was out to prove that the award of his county cap was no fluke. Geoff Cook and Roy Virgin were settled as an opening pair and, with players of the ability of Mushtaq, David Steele and Peter Willey and provided that everyone was fit, Wayne was unlikely to bat higher than number six in the order. He needed certainly to justify the County's faith in him. In May, Northants travelled to Chelmsford for a preliminary round Benson & Hedges match against Essex. The Saturday was washed out by rain, but on the Monday, Mushtaq won the toss and put Essex in to bat. On a damp seaming pitch the hosts lost seven wickets for 48 runs before slow left-arm bowler Ray East and wicketkeeper Neil Smith pulled them round with an eighth wicket stand of 109, so that they finally reached a total of 187. Wayne was on at first change and bowled his statutory eleven overs taking three wickets, all in the top order, for 13 runs. When it was Northants' turn to bat they slumped to 20 for 2 wickets before bad light carried the game into its third day. On the following morning Roy Virgin was out quickly before Mushtaq and Wayne came together to add 165 in an unbroken partnership to win the match by seven wickets, breaking in the process what was then the competition record for the fourth wicket. Wayne's 73 not out, together with his fine bowling, earned him his first Gold Award and Northants sailed into the quarter-finals of the Benson & Hedges Cup for the first time in their history.

The County's Championship form did not match their efforts of the previous season. Wayne weighed in with a second innings 110 against Yorkshire at Bradford, hitting sixteen boundaries in a knock lasting 213 minutes. The County might have won but eventually lost the match by six wickets. Wayne found his form again with another ton in the match against Kent at Wantage Road, his 103 not out in the first innings allowing the County to reach 355 for 5 wickets and to win the match convincingly by 54 runs. Unfortunately his performances were still somewhat inconsistent.

It is easy to forget that half of a county's programme is spent away from home and players often need to pair off and share rooms in hotels. For a period of some seven years Wayne and Peter Willey roomed together. Similar people they certainly were not. Peter, a Geordie through and through, had joined the County in 1966 at the age of sixteen, and in the 1976 season he had played the first two of his twenty-six Test matches for England in the series against the West Indies. He had always recognised that success needed to be earned and had originally sought to bowl medium pace in support of his outstanding batting. When his knees started to cause him trouble he turned to off-spin and did this well enough to be called on to bowl for England from time to time. He recalls nowadays how his father said to him at an early age: 'Practise everything, leg spinners, off spinners, you don't know when they might come in handy.' He now is glad that he did just that. People say that opposites attract and it is remarkable how well Wayne and Peter Willey got on together. 'Larky was going to bed when I was getting up,' Peter now recalls, but the two of them had a good

Northamptonshire CCC, 1977. From left to right, back row: Bob Cottam, Peter Willey, Alan Hodgson, George Sharp, John Dye, Geoff Cook, David Steele. Front row: Sarfraz Nawaz, Bishen Bedi, Mushtaq Mohammad (captain), Jim Yardley, Wayne Larkins.

understanding – namely, that Wayne would come in quietly after a night out, which was often the case, and that Peter would get up without disturbing Wayne on the following morning. 'Larky was one of those lucky blokes,' Peter now muses. 'He could go drinking all night and be as fresh as a daisy the next day. The way he drank would have killed anyone else, but he was a superb athlete and never let it affect his form.'

Wayne's sleeping habits did, however, have an amusing consequence when the County were at New Road, Worcester in July 1977. Wayne had, as usual, come back late to his room at the Gifford Hotel on the second night of the match. Northants had secured a sound first innings lead, but the last day was obviously going to be something of a nail-biter. Peter Willey had gone down to breakfast, taken a walk round the cathedral at about half past eight and then set off for the ground, leaving Wayne asleep and assuming that his alarm clock had been correctly set. But no such luck for Wayne! At about ten minutes before play was due to start George Sharp, the Northants wicketkeeper, looked around the dressing room and said: 'Where's Ned?' He certainly was not there. A phone call from George to the hotel roused him and he set off for the ground carrying all his kit since, as the match was due to end that day, he would not be returning to the hotel. As he approached the bridge over the River Severn from which you can look down over the ground, he saw Mushtaq leading the Northants team on to the pitch. Taking the view that one might as well be hanged for a sheep as a lamb, Wayne took out his ever-present packet of Silk Cut, lit a cigarette and watched the game for about ten minutes from the bridge. He then sloped off down to the pavilion, changed and joined the team on the field. A few of the team were grumbling, others laughing and pulling his leg, but the episode seemed largely to be forgotten as Bishen Bedi and Peter Willey made inroads into the Worcester second innings, finally dismissing them for 256 and leaving Northants some 184 runs to win.

Wayne admits to having kept a low profile at lunchtime, after which Northants got off to a sound start with Geoff Cook scoring an excellent 67. They were, however, in dire trouble at 160 for 6, Wayne being fifth out when he skied Norman Gifford and was caught and bowled for a single. His heroics of the previous season against Worcester were certainly not repeated! Mushtaq, however, played a captain's knock of 63 not out and the County got home by four wickets. However, the skipper was incensed with his side's feeble batting in the middle order and immediately called them all into the dressing room so that he could give them the rollicking he felt they deserved. For the second time in the day Wayne was AWOL, having enjoyed a thoroughly leisurely bath. At the end of Mushtaq's stern team-talk Wayne, totally unaware, strolled into the dressing room covered with nothing more than a towel and sat down next to his skipper. 'Well played, Mush,' he uttered. 'Thanks, Ned,' was the reply. As Wayne now recalls: 'Roy Virgin and Steely and several others were absolutely fuming.'

At the end of the 1977 season Northants had dropped from second to ninth in the Championship, were bottom in the Sunday League and had made only a moderate showing in the two other competitions. Their best performance was reaching the semi-final of the Benson & Hedges Cup where they went down by five runs to Kent in a tightly fought encounter. There were, however, stirrings in the camp back at Wantage

Wayne in 1977, aged twenty-three. (Bill Smith)

Wayne batting in the 1977 season. (Bob Thomas)

Road. A dinner scheduled for May 1977 to celebrate the successes of the previous season had not gone as planned and the players had threatened to boycott it owing to inadequate bonus payments. As it happened, the delay in the Essex Benson & Hedges tie, where Wayne had won the Gold Award, meant that they would have missed it anyway, but the important piece of news was that Kerry Packer, the Australian TV magnate, had signed up most of the world's leading cricketers for his World Series. Among these players was Mushtaq, who had not mentioned the matter to the Northants Committee. The Committee decided, therefore, to embark on a change of course. John Dye, the left-arm pace bowler who had sought to find a lucrative contract for Wayne in Rhodesia, was released, while Bishen Bedi was sacked, which led to a protracted industrial dispute which the club won owing to the skill of their solicitor and the calm evidence of Dennis Brookes. Then, at the end of the season, Mushtaq and Roy Virgin were sent on their way. Ken Turner, the secretary, had been working behind the scenes and had heard that Jim Watts had now qualified as a teacher and would like to return to first-class cricket. After the spilling of much blood and some rowdy extraordinary general meetings at Wantage Road, Jim Watts was re-appointed for his second stint as skipper for the 1978 season.

While Mushtaq had supported Wayne up hill and down dale and had even turned a blind eye to some of his foibles, as the Worcester match had proved, the appointment of the schoolmasterly Jim Watts was a blessing in disguise. Roy Virgin had left the County and there was now a space at the top of the order as Geoff Cook's partner. Jim had broached with Wayne the question of opening some seasons previously, but now his plan went into operation. Thus was forged a partnership lasting twelve seasons, which came to be recognised as the outstanding one of that era.

If only someone in the Northants establishment had realised earlier what opening the batting would do for Wayne! He took to the task with such determination and flair that success became a way of life. Wayne's masterly 107 against Nottinghamshire in his first outing as Geoff Cook's partner was followed in June by 170 not out against Worcestershire when he batted throughout the 100 overs of the Northants innings. Geoffrey Moorhouse in *The Best Loved Game* gives a magnificent account of Wayne's batting in this innings, perhaps his first really great one:

> *There is a fiction that Championship matches start at a snail's pace because they feel they have so much time in hand, but Cook and Larkins are soon giving a lie to that. Almost a run a minute comes in the first half-hour as those men in maroon caps seek to assert themselves against the Worcestershire attack. Cook, having edged a boundary to get off the mark, is the more careful of the two, but Larkins is unbridled from the first ball he receives. He plays and misses Pridgeon once or twice, but is not put off by this and turns the bowler off his legs for 4, then square-cuts Holder beautifully to the fence. Within the hour the batsmen are up with the clock and the West Stand sages assert that this is a quite reasonable start, as Norman Gifford rearranges his bowling to take the ascendancy away from Northants. Holder gives way to Cumbes and Pridgeon changes ends ... But people are still sauntering into the ground with their shopping bags laden with thermos and sandwiches. I think it is perhaps the spectators who give Championship cricket a leisurely name. Cumbes labours for a while from the pavilion end, but in the twenty-fourth over Holder is brought back and the first drama of the match occurs. The West Indian's third ball flies off the edge of Larkins's bat straight into the cupped hands of Turner at slip - and falls to the ground. Holder's hands go to his hips in frustration, but his shoulders are resigned ... A few minutes later, the Worcestershire spirits rise again when Cook, impatient with his own cautious rate, swings at Pridgeon and is caught by Humphries behind.*
>
> *'It'll slow up now', says someone, cocking his eye at the scoreboard's 79 for 1, as Steele's bare head bobs down the pavilion steps. Steele may have been going through a bad patch of late, but there is still something in his approach to the wicket that would hearten any team in need of runs. Thus he watches Larkins defend for a few balls, practising his own strokes on the side each time the bowler returns; when his own turn comes he tries to get Holder away to leg several times, but mostly he is going forward to stifle the ball ... Then Steele dabs at another delivery ... This dab flicks the ball to Hemsley, who takes it at the second attempt low down in the slips ... Larkins has prospered all this time, however, and with his own score, Northamptonshire's has steadily grown. When the cricketers go in to lunch, the two fallen wickets have been exchanged for 122 runs and Larkins stands at 70 not out ... Lunch over, Larkins moves on, the tiny figure of Williams strives, and Gifford again manipulates his bowling to maintain any distraction that the meal break may have begun ... Larkins has reached 92, and since being missed by Turner, he has done nothing dangerously wrong. Almost every over has added to his score and the longer he is there the more commanding he looks. But now a strange pause interrupts his progress towards the century. It takes him one hour and five minutes to move from 92 to 99 and impatience*

begins to rustle round the County Ground. There is no slow hand-clapping for Wayne Larkins of Bedfordshire belongs to Northants; he is being given the benefit of all East Midland doubts, but the impulse to jeer is evidently there. This is misplaced, for the central drama of cricket is emphazised in Larkins's present plight.

From the boundary today it is hard to see any difference in the playing of the pitch between 2.45 and 3.50. The bowling of Gifford and Patel, Holder, Pridgeon and Cumbes appears to be no more tantalizing, no more hostile when Larkins is clearly struggling to defend his wicket than when he is clumping the bowlers aggressively to the ropes. While he is making these seven agonized runs, Willey comes out, knocks up a useful 24 and departs again, and Yardley settles down to some ebullient strokes ... The nervous nineties surely plagued anyone no more than this, and the defiance of the batsman was never more tortured to behold. From a cavalier charge as Rupert of the Rhine, poor Larkins has suddenly been translated into Horatius at the Bridge, and the Etruscans of Worcestershire are hemming him in. At the striker's end Larkins crouches ... as Gifford's delivery pitches fractionally short in a temptingly fulsome arc and turns towards the leg-stump in its upward bounce, Larkins steps forward, left elbow high, bat utterly straight ... and brings the blade down at a precise angle which sends the ball gently along the ground to where mid-off was waiting for a catch. So the duel between batsman and bowler, the drama of cricket, goes on.

Then suddenly he strikes Holder away for two runs, at 3.56, and he has his century at last. Having painfully struggled through those last few runs he now becomes a different man, even more cavalier than when he plundered the bowling up to 92. He has passed through a psychological barrier ... After tea Larkins takes the Worcestershire bowlers one by one and pays them back crushingly for the confinement they had earlier imposed. In just fifteen minutes straddling five o'clock, he hits 35 runs as he rushes from 125 to 160 ... As almost every local knows Larkins is approaching the highest score of his life, the 167 he got against Warwickshire a couple of seasons ago. Will he better it now...but Worcester are not going to present Larkins with his records on a plate and they have him fidgeting again as he goes for those last few runs. He gets them, though, and when Northants go in at 312 for 4 he is still unbeaten with 170 in the book.

This elegant and somewhat poetic piece of writing sums up Wayne at this stage of his life. All the talent was there, but when the challenge came there was something missing. It had plagued him when he first appeared at Wantage Road, it took immense time for him to bridge the gap between First XI and Second XI cricket and it was still to cause him trouble when he appeared for England or in crunch matches at venues like Lord's. There have always been sportsmen with these sorts of difficulties and they have always needed guidance. Was this guidance available in the establishment at Northants or in the high echelons of England cricket? In spite of this hindrance, Wayne ended his season with 3 tons, 5 fifties and 1,343 runs in Championship matches, more than any other Northants player.

Even more exciting was Wayne's performance against Surrey in the John Player League match in July at Tring. Surrey had notched up 179 in their 40 overs and Northants had slumped to 57 for 4 when Wayne came to the wicket. He proceeded to hit an unbeaten 107 in 74 minutes with 8 sixes and 8 fours to get the County home by five wickets with eight balls to spare. David Steele, who had joined Wayne with the score on 107 for 5, contributed a modest 6 not out. The excitement of the match and its ending is encapsulated by Wayne's friend, Richard Peel, a reporter at that time for the *Chronicle & Echo* in Northampton:

There was a feeling of utter incredulity among spectators when they left the tiny Tring ground. Have Northants really won? Did Wayne Larkins really hit all those sixes? It is hard to believe. No gambling man would have put a penny on Northants reaching 180 at the halfway stage, but Larkins suddenly changed from a Dr Jekyll to a mean Mr Hyde. After treating the spin of Intikhab Alam and Pat Pocock with ultra respect he went on a sensational run spree. He smote 8 mighty sixes and hammered as many fours. With five overs to go Northants needed 50 to win, but the 36th over was the turning point. Larkins hit a four and a hat trick of sixes off Roger Knight who shouted 'Oh, sorry!' to his fellow fielders when he realised that his fourth delivery was a juicy full toss.

More significant than his success for Northants was the fact that Wayne was asked to turn out for MCC against the Pakistan touring team in May and for Young England against New Zealand in August. Sadly, as always seemed to happen when facing a new environment and challenge, Wayne did not make the most of his chances. Referring to his form in the Young England match at Leicester, Wayne said: 'I wasn't nervous or anything. It was just one of those occasions when things did not work out properly.' Although he did not make the most of these opportunities for representative cricket the sporting press plugged Wayne for inclusion in the one-day international matches against Pakistan in the first half of the split season and for the Tests against New Zealand in the second half. Nothing came of their urgings, but they continued to put Wayne's name forward for the winter tour of Australia under Mike Brearley's leadership. 'I don't think about it,' Wayne said at the time. 'It's every player's ultimate goal, but until it happens it will just be a dream.' There were a number of young players in the minds of England's selectors at this time. Wayne was certainly one, together with Mike Gatting, Chris Tavaré, Graham Gooch and David Gower. In the end Geoff Boycott, Mike Brearley and Graham Gooch got the openers' slots while David Gower also received the selectors' nod.

While Wayne failed to be selected for England's touring party, there was some better news on the horizon. He was asked to keep the news secret until final arrangements had been made with the sponsors, but he heard fairly soon after the announcement of the team that he had been selected for a Whitbread Scholarship in Australia along with Mike Gatting, Jonathan Agnew and Chris Tavaré. He and Mike would be going to Sydney to play Grade Cricket for the Sutherland and Balmain clubs respectively, while Chris would play in Perth. All three would be reserves for the England touring party. 'I was asked first whether I would be available and, although I said that it came as something of a surprise, it was really tremendous news,' Wayne told the press. He saw very sensibly that time in Australia close to the England touring party would broaden his experience, keep him in the selectors' eye and create the chance to play on different and, probably, better wickets than he was used to at home. Alec Bedser, the Chairman of England's Selectors, commented at the time: 'We have been keeping an eye on Larkins for some time', but several of Wayne's colleagues at Northampton, notably David Steele, wondered why there was a need to keep an eye on him. Why not pick him? After all, Wayne was rising twenty-five and most Test playing countries do not wait even until that age to blood players of class. But Wayne remained the victim of the English system of selection which has served the country so badly over the years. Players seem to remain pawns on the selectors' chessboard to be selected and then dropped almost at a whim, to find out their fate on the car radio as they drive to the Sunday League match or, even worse, to hear it from the gateman as they arrive at the ground. 'He will be on hand if we need him for the Tests,' Mr Bedser concluded. The arch-conservatism

Wayne square cuts to the boundary. (George Herringshaw: www.sporting-heroes.net)

of the selectors at this time is hard to fathom. Their failure to see the need to blood young players of real promise led to their choosing Clive Radley of Middlesex for the tour. As a player whose home ground was Lord's, he stood a better chance than Wayne from the unfashionable cricketing backwater of Northamptonshire, but he was aged thirty-four at the start of the tour and ended up by not being selected for a Test match and scoring 138 first-class runs at an average of 15. Who knows what Wayne might have achieved? His electrifying fielding would at least have been a boon.

On Boxing Day 1978, Wayne flew to Sydney. He was immediately well received by the Sutherland Club and soon found himself opening the batting at the Caringbah Oval with

Andrew Hilditch, the so-called 'happy hooker', a title he had gained for no reason other than his innocent propensity to get caught at long leg while attacking bouncers. Wayne's belligerent batting and his genial approach off the field soon caught the imagination of the local cricket fans and it was not long before he had acquired the nickname *Larrikins,* a rogue in the Australian vernacular. Warwick Hadfield, the well-known Australian cricket journalist, gave an impression of Wayne's performance down under:

> *Not until you have heard the softer accent does it become apparent that the hard-hitting, sun-tanned opener beneath the sky-blue Sutherland cap hails from parts other than Cronella Beach. The affable Northamptonshire batsman has come to join Sutherland for the second half of the southern summer. He has adapted as quickly to the wickets as he has to the Antipodean life style and, despite damage to a hand inflicted by speedster Geoff Lawson, he has stamped his class on the Grade side. His professional approach has been an illuminating experience to his Sutherland team-mates and his influence on the whole side, which until his arrival was languishing in the middle of the points table, has been clearly visible. Sutherland ended the season in fine style when Larrikins and his partner Wayne Moodie produced a club record opening stand of 124 to allow their side to declare at 202 for four wickets in only 133 minutes against Mossman. Spectators and fielders abandoned the search after he sent one ball soaring over mid-wicket towards the waters of Middle Harbour and one graceful square cut had old timers shaking their heads after the ball had been retrieved from the pickets. Until I saw Asif Iqbal's hundred against Australia in Perth I ranked this innings as the finest I had seen all summer. In a season of dry and uninspired batting Larrikins' truculent efforts have been as welcome as freshet in the outback.*

Wayne felt pleased with his efforts too: 'If the ball is there to be hit, I like to hit it. It does not matter whether it is the first ball or you are past your hundred.' The philosophy of playing the ball and not the bowler had become by this time very much part of Wayne's way of playing cricket. Some bowlers thanked their lucky stars if they did not have to open up against Wayne. Jonathan Agnew recalls a match at Grace Road, Leicester, when Wayne drilled his first ball through the covers for four, 'grinning broadly behind his bristling moustache as he did so' and then smashing the second over cover's head, high over the George Geary Stand and down the Milligan Road for six. He coined the phrase 'being Nedded', which became current on the county circuit over a number of years. Nor was Jonathan the only bowler to confess some dread at the thought of taking the new ball to Wayne.

The Sutherland club secretary, John Smythe, expressed what was clearly a universal view that Wayne's services should be re-engaged for the following Australian season, although he saw very clearly that his own club captain, Andrew Hilditch, and Wayne could be on opposing sides in future Anglo-Australian encounters. 'The success this season of *Ditch* and *Larrikins* could become a deciding factor next year in blunting the respective opening attacks,' Smythe said.

The three months that Wayne spent in Australia in the first part of 1979 was of obvious benefit to his experience of playing cricket under conditions very different from those in England, but it gave him a greater confidence which had the potential to turn this likeable, but hesitant, young cricketer 'with the apologetic persona', as one of his captains put it, into a truly great Test batsman. In spite of this, the ball was mainly in Wayne's court. Would he be able to discipline himself and firm up his confidence to fulfil his potential? The coming season might be the key.

5
RECOGNITION AT LAST

Wayne boomeranged back from Australia sun-tanned and enthusiastic, but with a broken thumb, courtesy of Geoff Lawson, Australia's aspiring quick bowler. He was possibly wiser as a man and certainly more experienced in the Aussie way of cricket and their determined attitude to the game. Although he had not scored a ton during his four months down under, he had ended his stay with an average of 46, had seen England performing in two Tests and had watched some of the Kerry Packer games. He was pleased to get back to see Jane, who had not been able to accompany him owing to the uncertainty about retaining her job with the firm of solicitors, Shoosmith and Harrison.

The main highlight of the first part of the 1979 English season was the Prudential Cup and there was much press speculation about Wayne's chances of reaching the England squad. His form for Northants at the start of the season was not outstanding, but at the end of May he scored an excellent 93 against Surrey under the nose of Test selector Ken Barrington, while Alec Bedser, the Chairman of Selectors, was heard to comment that Wayne had been close, but not quite close enough, to being included the previous winter. On the Saturday prior to the announcement of the squad, Northants were at Worcester and Wayne top-scored with 51 in the county match. As was always the way, the news of the selectors' deliberations came over the radio at Sunday lunchtime and, as Wayne walked from the Gifford Hotel over the bridge to the ground to start the Sunday League match, he was pounced upon by the Northampton press who had been lying in wait for him. They had told him the good news that he had been included in Mr Bedser's squad of fourteen players to contest the Prudential World Cup. Wayne had obviously thought that he was in with a chance, but when the news came he was certainly elated, but genuinely modest about his success and somewhat dazed. 'It will take a while to sink in; my heart is fluttering a bit,' he said, although some people could be forgiven for thinking that the palpitations were the result of the amount he had drunk the previous evening.

England's first match was at Lord's against Australia and it was perhaps unsurprising that skipper Mike Brearley and Geoff Boycott took the opening slots against the old enemy in a match which England won comfortably by six wickets. The next match was against minnows Canada at Old Trafford and a chance was missed to blood Wayne against lesser opposition, an almost predictably conservative decision from England's selectors. He did not get a game against Pakistan either, but England won again and moved into the semi-finals. One can almost sense the selectors' approach to the problem. Derek Randall had had three poor matches at first wicket down; now, when the going was about to get really tough in the semis, here was the chance to bring in a tyro! Out of position and in an arguably tough spot at number three, as the old firm of Brearley and Boycott were still opening, Wayne opened his international career confidently, but rather rashly and was caught in the covers for 7. He did not get to bowl either; Mike Brearley was clearly saving him for the final! The powerful West Indian side had, of course, surged into the final with some impressive victories and Wayne found himself before 25,000 spectators with many more locked out of Lord's and in a side that was going into a limited overs match with only four recognised bowlers. It appeared that the selectors were intending to reinforce the batting and hope that Geoff Boycott, Wayne and Graham Gooch would make up the fifth bowler. While it is true that Gooch and Boycott had conceded a mere thirty-two runs in the semi-final against New Zealand, this match was now against the powerful West Indies. It proved to be a calamitous misjudgement and had the predictable consequences. Although Derek Randall ran out Gordon Greenidge with some electrifying fielding and Mike Hendrick and Chris Old did some damage to the West Indian middle order, a fifth wicket partnership of 139 between the incomparable Viv Richards and Collis King allowed their side to reach 286 for 9 wickets in their sixty overs. Had Wayne expected to bowl? 'Mike Brearley merely said I might be used. I had not bowled much for the County this year, but he came over and asked what field I wanted.' Wayne's two overs went for 21 runs and the 'fifth bowler' combination conceded 86 wicketless runs to the West Indies total. Wayne had, in fact, bowled a mere 17 overs in limited overs cricket prior to the final and taken 2 wickets. It was another piece of 'it will be all right on the night' decision-making by England's thoughtless selectors. When it was England's turn to bat, Boycott required seventeen overs to reach double figures and, although he and Brearley put on 129 for the first wicket, by the time they were both out England needed 158 from 22 overs. Wayne, who had been pencilled in for the number three slot, found himself, owing to the slow start, gradually pushed further and further down the order until he finally went in at number seven, only to be bowled by Joel Garner for a duck. Unhappiness all round! England reached a modest 194 in 51 overs and lost by 92 runs.

Two interesting vignettes, however, come out of this match which was a dismal occasion for Wayne, although he sensibly did not let it show. Among the VIP spectators at Lord's was David Wilson, who had coached Wayne at the Bushmead School and helped him into the junior Huntingdon side, and David recalls Wayne's particular kindness when he presented him after the match with a miniature bat autographed by the two teams. The second story occurs nearly twenty years later. England are playing South Africa in the Fifth and deciding Test at Leeds in August 1998. As Nasser Hussain, battling hard in England's second innings, pushes Pollock's slower ball to mid-off to end a seven-hour stint six runs short of his century, 'head down, wiping away the tears and oblivious to the standing ovation' as *Wisden* described it, the radio commentator is heard to mutter: 'I have never seen a man leave a cricket field in a more dejected state since the time when I saw Wayne Larkins yorked by Garner and leaving the Lord's pitch in the 1979 World Cup final.' The jocular remarks to the press at the time of 'I just did not see it' were, of course, just a cover. Wayne Larkins, for all his apparent laid-back bonhomie, was starting to care passionately about his cricket.

After the conclusion of the Prudential Cup, England were entertaining India as their summer guests and the visitors' first match was against Northants at Wantage Road. Wayne chipped in with a good 51 in the first innings and soon found himself back at Lord's in the MCC side to meet the tourists again. Unfortunately the big match occasion overcame him again and he did little with the bat. This misfortune was compounded by his little finger being broken by Karsan Ghavri, the Indian left-arm pace bowler. This took him out of circulation for a few matches and automatically out of contention for a First Test place.

England started the series against India with an innings win and they performed creditably in the Second and Third Tests, but by the time of the Fourth Test at the Oval at the end of August, the selectors were unhappy with Derek Randall's form and called Wayne into the team for what he hoped would be his first real Test match. Just prior to the Test, Northants had played Sussex at Hove for a place in the Gillette final and Wayne had managed to get hit on the hand again, this time by Imran Khan. Insult was added to injury when Richard Williams called Wayne for a quick single and Paul Parker, with one stump to aim at, ran him out for a modest 11. When he returned to the dressing room his hand was sore and a hospital x-ray showed that it was broken between the wrist and the little finger. Wayne was keen to declare himself fit for the Test, but Jim Watts was against his playing and Ken Turner advised him to withdraw, suggesting that he would not do himself justice. It was a shame, and Alan Butcher from Surrey was called into the England side for his one and only Test match. The event did, however, have an ironic twist to it. The Northants establishment, despite having counselled Wayne to withdraw from the Test Match, still included him in the County's team to play Essex at Chelmsford, where on the Wednesday preceding the start of the Test, Wayne had scored an excellent 91 in the first innings. Even worse, he was asked to bowl nine overs in the Essex innings. It was poor advice to a young cricketer, who still needed a great deal of guidance, and it is difficult to see how he could have accepted it. Strangely enough, the selectors said nothing either.

Things had looked up at Wantage Road during the course of the season. They now had in place a top batting order of real ability, the so-called 'Famous Five' of Geoff Cook, Wayne Larkins, Richard 'Chippy' Williams, Peter Willey and and Allan Lamb, a South African batsman from Western Province who had qualified for the County at the start of the 1979 season and was to play an important part in the affairs of both England and Northants in the 1980s. Players at the club such as Tim Lamb, who had started his career at Middlesex, moved to Northants in 1978 and is now secretary to the England and Wales Cricket Board, have commented that, in those days, Northants were set tougher fourth innings totals because of the strength of their first five batsmen. The County also improved on their poor showing of the previous season and finished eleventh in the Championship. Allan Lamb was everyone's toast and ended the season with over 1,600 runs at an average in excess of 60, but, apart from Geoff Cook who also recorded 1,000 runs, Wayne was next up and just failed to reach the four figure target in the Championship. An average of 45 and three hundreds were not, however, a bad return for a season's work.

Furthermore he played a brilliant innings in the Sunday League match against Leicestershire, when he scored 111 in 36 overs and put on 202 for the first wicket with Peter Willey, who also reached three figures. The County's one-day form was also excellent and they reached the final of the Gillette Cup, although they lost by 45 runs to Somerset. Wayne was claimed a second time by Joel Garner, this time lbw for another duck. It had been a season of sound, but unspectacular, progress for him, but better things were in sight.

Wayne heard at the end of the season that he had been awarded the Lord's Taverners-Schweppes Prize of £500 for the best batsman aged twenty-five and under and he and Jane had a pleasant trip to the London Hilton as a result. But the real news that everyone in Northampton was waiting for was whether Wayne and Peter Willey were going to make the England party which was touring Australia for a second winter in succession under the captaincy of Mike Brearley. It was, thankfully, good news. Both had been included and Wayne had appeared to leapfrog over Chris Tavaré, Mike Gatting, Bob Woolmer, Brian

Rose and sundry other England batting hopefuls. Fame brought tangible rewards too: Wayne and Peter soon found themselves being presented with Austin Princess cars by a British Leyland dealership.

After he and Jane had taken a short holiday on the South Coast, Wayne set about preparing for the tour to Australia, which was beginning in November. Things were fitting nicely into place for him and just before the team left Heathrow they were all invited by the Prime Minister, Margaret Thatcher, for a good luck drink; 9 Ford Lane to 10 Downing Street was pretty good going. 'The adrenaline is beginning to flow now,' Wayne is quoted as saying at the time. 'I suppose I am getting excited as we are getting close to leaving. It is really the fulfilment of a life's ambition.' It would be a demanding tour, too, with twenty-three hotel changes and some of the travelling done as soon as day-night games ended. Yet, as the tour became a reality, Wayne was to find that the justifiable pride in his achievements was to take some dents in the months ahead.

Wayne knew that he was not in the first choice team when England landed in Australia in November, although he reckoned, with some justification, that he was the number three opening bat and would be drafted in if an injury occurred to Boycott or Brearley. He was left out of the first match, but was part of England's victory in a one-dayer against Northern New South Wales. Here he batted with Geoff Boycott as they chased a mere 136 for victory

The England team which toured Australia and India in 1979/80. From left to right, back row: Bernard Thomas (physiotherapist), Wayne Larkins, Graham Stevenson, John Lever, Peter Willey, Graham Dilley, John Emburey, Graham Gooch, David Gower, Derek Randall, David Bairstow, Geoffrey Saulez (scorer). Front row: Alec Bedser (manager), Derek Underwood, Ian Botham, Mike Brearley (captain), Geoff Boycott, Bob Taylor, Ken Barrington (assistant manager). (Bristol Photos Bombay)

and the Old Master outscored Wayne by a large margin. This was perhaps not surprising as Geoff managed to hog the bowling for a whole ten overs in the middle of the innings, while Wayne did not face one single ball. He was not given a chance to play in the first of the one-day internationals as Derek Randall was brought in to open when Geoff Boycott was injured. And so it continued until after Christmas. Although Wayne played in the occasional state match and batted in various positions, it was not until January that he was paired with Graham Gooch to open against Australia in a day-nighter in Sydney. He did keep his place in the remaining one-dayers and even played in the two finals against West Indies, both of which England lost. He was, however, moved around in the batting order like a yo-yo and, rather predictably, he did not make much of an impression.

Because of the elaborate one-day programme, the Test matches were restricted to three games on this tour. In the first two games Derek Randall and then Graham Gooch were Boycott's opening partners, but after a splendid 90 against New South Wales, Wayne finally played in his first Test. He had not found the going easy up till then, but he did make himself highly popular with young people in Canberra during the New South Wales game by standing for forty-five minutes at the head of a queue some thirty yards long, signing autographs and being congratulated for doing so over the loudspeaker system. 'We would like to thank Mr Larkins for his kindness to the children here today.' Essentially, though, he was feeling adrift. 'There have been times when I wondered quite what I was doing here, but now the waiting is well worthwhile.' he said proudly at the time. 'Playing for your country is always worth waiting for. What I need is confidence and that means getting through the first thirty or forty minutes, which won't be easy. If I can do that I reckon I can do well.' Filling the number three slot Wayne fulfilled some of his intentions by scoring 25 in a good partnership with Graham Gooch in the first innings, but he did less well in the second, where, despite an excellent hundred from Ian Botham, England failed to stop Australia winning all three Tests. After Australia, the England side called in to play India in the Golden Jubilee Test at Bombay. In a match which England won comfortably by ten wickets, Wayne kept his number three place, but fell lbw to Ghavri for a duck. Never one to complain, Wayne nowadays points out with a rueful grin from under the bushy moustache that the ball 'would easily have missed another set.'

By this time Jane had come out to Sydney and together they stayed with friends from his time with Sutherland. 'Larrikins' played a few matches for his adopted club, before they had to return to England for the 1980 season. The start to Wayne's international career had not been covered in glory. Two hand injuries, a few cases of bad umpiring and some odd decisions and poor man-management by England's selectors had not helped the shy and insecure young batsman to prosper. On the other hand, others will say that Wayne did not always help himself. There is no doubt that he fell foul of the England management on the Australia tour and this may have prejudiced, rather unjustly considering their own obvious failings, the course of his later career. Spending excessive time in amusement arcades with Graham Stevenson, drinking 'tinnies' with friends on top of the Melbourne scorebox when he was twelfth man in a one-day match against Australia and keeping the coach waiting after a night-out, which ended at 5.00 a.m., in the Bourbon and Beefsteak in Sydney's King's Cross after another one-day international did not endear him to Mr Bedser or even to the more sympathetic Mike Brearley.

1980 was, however, another season. Wayne was in the England set-up and the West Indies were England's next Test opponents. The lights had been dimmed a little, but the future remained essentially bright.

6

THE SELECTORS' CHESSBOARD

England had returned from a disappointing tour of Australia and India, but Wayne and Peter Willey were welcomed back in Northampton like heroes. A local brewery donated 2,016 pints, that is to say seven barrels, to each of them on their return. 'Mine lasted a lot longer than Larky's did,' Peter commented later.

The Packer furore, occasioned in 1977 when Tony Greig, then England captain, took some of the country's leading cricketers off to join Kerry Packer's media empire in Australia, had been settled in the off-season. It meant, therefore, that players such as Dennis Amiss, Bob Woolmer, Alan Knott and Derek Underwood were again available for selection for the national side. Notwithstanding this, Peter and Wayne had every reason to believe that they were men in possession and would come into close reckoning when it came to the Prudential one-day and the Test matches against the touring West Indians. Wayne, in particular, had done well in a curtain-raiser against the tourists at Milton Keynes and his scores for the County team, captained for his last season by Jim Watts, had been excellent. It was, therefore, yet another disappointment for Wayne to learn that, while Peter had made the side for the Prudential matches, he himself had again been omitted. David Lloyd of Lancashire, now aged thity-three, who had batted tolerably well for his county at the start of the season, but who had been so shell-shocked by the thunderbolts delivered by Dennis Lillee and Jeff Thomson on the 1974/75 tour of Australia, had been recalled to bat at number seven against the West Indian fast bowlers, while Chris Tavaré of Kent with sound, but not outstanding, one-day form had been handed his debut. Any idea of continuity in team selection seemed to be absent. Wayne, as the man in possession, must have found this incredibly confusing. 'I learned a lot in the one-day games down under last winter and I have been very happy with my form this summer. Oh well!' There was probably little more he could say considering the selectors' urge to tinker with England sides without their having any clear idea of building a team.

Wayne did not get a look-in for either of the first two Test matches at Trent Bridge and Lord's but, having made a quick hundred against Glamorgan in early June and a scintillating 127 with 20 fours against Gloucestershire, he reached his 1,000 runs by the end of June. England had narrowly lost the First Test and they had hung on a for a draw in the second, but the selectors were concerned about the problems created by the West Indies' fast bowling battery of Roberts, Garner, Holding and Croft. They came up, therefore, with their own unique solution – play four opening batsmen at the top of the England order! Graham Gooch and Geoff Boycott were retained as openers, but Chris Tavaré and Bob Woolmer were jettisoned in favour of Brian Rose of Somerset and Wayne, batting at number three and four, for the Third Test at Old Trafford. Wayne had obviously thought about the prospect of Roberts and company and noted: 'It does not matter when you go in against their attack; it is always like opening the innings. I like playing fast bowling, but they are bombarding you all the time, so the hardest thing is to stay in long enough to get used to their pace. If you average it out you only get about one bad ball every three overs and it is important not to miss it and to put it away for four.' The unusual selectorial stratagem and England's sterling batting meant that they were able to hold their opponents at bay for the rest of the series in the games at the Oval and Headingley. Wayne managed only 90 runs in six innings, but he had grafted well in an unusual position. Some would say that one cannot expect a batsman to perform to his best if he is batting out of position; others, like George Sharp, Wayne's colleague at Northampton, say clearly: 'If you are picked for England to bat at number four, you bat at number four!' Once again, it had been a relatively unhappy experience for Wayne. Keith Andrew, his mentor of some years previously, had always taken the view that Wayne had a habit of putting his leg down the pitch as the ball was being bowled. He clearly had a desire to get into line, but it often meant that he was playing across his front leg. It was something which he had to work hard at in the nets and it is interesting to note that the very same fault caused Graham Gooch considerable trouble, even quite late in his career, especially when he was playing Terry Alderman, the Australian opening bowler. Wayne never found it easy to accept criticism, but his pride in his cricket caused him to work hard and think closely how to eliminate the faults in his technique which were showing up at this higher level.

Wayne's form for the County remained at a remarkably high standard. At the end of August he scored 156 in a second wicket partnership of 322 with Richard Williams against Leicestershire, a record stand for the County and one which included 49 boundaries. The County also made excellent progress in the Benson & Hedges Cup in which Wayne picked up a bowling hat-trick against the combined Oxford and Cambridge side and his second Gold Award with 108 against Warwickshire. He also saw the County home with 62 in the semi-final against Middlesex, where Jim Watts won an exciting captaincy duel with Mike Brearley – this was no mean feat. In July the County went on to win their second Lord's final when they narrowly overcame Essex in another exciting match. Geoff Cook was succeeding Jim Watts as captain in the coming season and some people were saying, now that the pace attack of Sarfraz Nawaz, Jim Griffiths and Tim Lamb was maturing to complement the batting strength of the 'Famous Five', that the County might well become the 'Team of the Eighties'. Engel and Radd, in their history of the County, are more cynical: 'In soccer, they were saying the same thing about Crystal Palace.'

In the 1980 season England, having drawn the Prudential matches with the West Indies and held them to four draws against one loss in the Test matches, now found that they had the unenviable task of entertaining the Australians for a few matches at the end of the season. The selectors decided that Wayne and Chris Tavaré had not achieved what they were seeking and Mike Gatting, Bill Athey from Yorkshire and Roland Butcher from Middlesex were drafted into the England middle order. The same players were also in the touring party, led by Ian Botham, to tour the West Indies during the winter. The inconsistency of the selectors' policy is hard to fathom, even now at a distance, but there may have been some attempt at political correctness in the selection of the black Roland Butcher for the West Indies tour. Wayne had scored over 1,500 runs in the Championship at an average of over 50 and nearly 1,800 runs altogether, including four tons, a performance that Athey, Gatting and Butcher in no way matched. Bill Athey had reached 1,110 runs at a low average of 33, while the other two were well short of their thousand runs. Picking players from 'fashionable' counties had always been part of the selectors'

Northamptonshire's 'Famous Five'. From top to bottom: Richard Williams, Peter Willey, Geoff Cook, Wayne Larkins, Allan Lamb. (Bob Thomas)

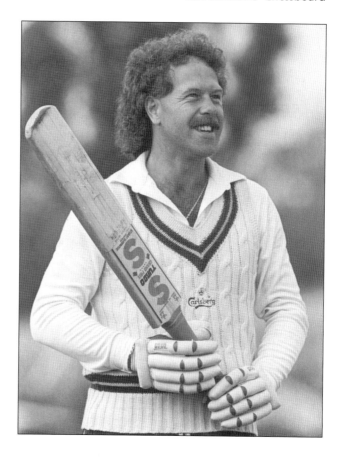

Wayne shows off his trusty 'Stuart Surridge' bat. (David Munden)

shenanigans and this occasion proved to be no exception.

After two interesting seasons in Australia, Wayne found himself unemployed for the winter. Work at the British Shoe Corporation and some semi-professional soccer was all he could look forward to. There is, perhaps, always a silver lining even to the darkest cloud and Wayne and Jane were able to start looking for a better house than their two-up, two-down in Church Street, Moulton. In fact they were able to move to a larger property in Hardingstone, just south of Northampton. There was further good news, for Jane was expecting their first child in May 1981.

1981 was going to be another Australian summer and all Wayne could do was to play well for the County and hope that he might again catch the selectors' eye. The winter tour to the West Indies had hardly been a roaring success. Although England had not been 'black-washed', as was the case some years later, and despite the fact that Graham Gooch, Geoff Boycott, David Gower and Peter Willey had all batted well, two Tests had been lost and two drawn. None of the middle order batsmen, such as Roland Butcher, Bill Athey and Mike Gatting had achieved anything of note, especially in the Test matches. Cynics at the time might have argued that Wayne had been better off out of it.

The 1981 Australian touring party, led by Kim Hughes, was probably not as strong as some to have reached these shores, but in Dennis Lillee and Terry Alderman they possessed an opening attack of immense power. For the Prudential Trophy one-day matches the England selectors were unable to resist further change and the Yorkshire batsman, Jim Love, found himself included in the line-up. The *Daily Mirror*, feeling an urge to misquote *Corinthians*, announced: 'Yorkshire have many promising young batsmen, but the greatest of these is Love.' They were not necessarily right. In the wicketkeeping area Paul Downton and David Bairstow, who had been members of the West Indies touring party, found themselves supplanted by Geoff Humpage from Warwickshire, whose batting was seen as excellent, but whose ability behind the stumps was unproven. It was the sort of ill-considered decision that has characterised the England selection process throughout the years and proved unfruitful because Humpage became so bogged down in the course of making 5 runs in the second match that Gatting, who had made 96, was forced into a rash stroke and England lost by two runs. After winning the first match England went down in the remaining three games and the First Test at Trent Bridge also recorded a loss. There was a draw in the Second Test at Lord's in which Ian Botham recorded a pair. He immediately resigned the England captaincy. Ian had been brought to the task far too early and it is intriguing to muse on what success in that capacity he might have had if he had been picked a little later. Mike Brearley was immediately summoned from retirement to take over the reins at Headingley, where Botham's amazing 149 not out and the eight Australian second innings wickets for 43 by Bob Willis brought an incredible 18-run victory for England. In the early afternoon people were glued to TV sets or radios, boys (and teachers!) did not return to class and offices and factories stopped work. 'Beauty and the Beast', the cerebral power of Brearley's leadership and the awesome power of Botham, drove England forward in the next two matches. The 5 wickets for 11 runs at Edgbaston and 118 at Old Trafford are only two of the heroic deeds by Botham in that August. By the time the sixth and final Test came to be played at the Oval, England's selectors were still not satisfied. A policy of continuous improvement may be sensible for the Ford Motor Company, but it is a different ball game when you are dealing with people and their careers. The old enemy was 3-1 down with one to play, but the selectors were unable to resist further change, this time, perhaps strangely, to Wayne's advantage.

Wayne had been enjoying another fruitful season for the County. At the beginning of June he took 157 off the Warwickshire attack at Edgbaston in an innings which included 2 sixes and 26 fours, an enormous 74 per cent in boundaries, and this was followed later in the month by his part in an exciting win at Derby over the home county. The home side lost a mere seven wickets in their two innings and, declaring twice, left Northants 276 to get at almost 90 runs an hour. With 37 off the four first overs, Geoff Cook and Wayne set about the bowling with such gusto that they reached 258 in two hours before Wayne departed for 126. In 53 overs the County had won by nine wickets – no wonder that other counties were mighty careful when setting Northants a fourth innings total to chase. In July, Wayne had been picked to play for a TCCB XI in a sort of Test trial against the second tourists of the season, the Sri Lankans, and at Trent Bridge he had scored a good 40 followed by a top score of 78 in the second knock. The form that Wayne was showing was not lost on anyone, not even Alec Bedser, who commented to the press: 'In-form batsman Wayne Larkins, if he keeps scoring runs, will be picked again for England. He is closer to recall than he may think.'

Despite the exhilaration of these three victories over the Australians, the England selectors still felt the urge to tinker. Apart from a 60-run opening partnership in the Second Test at Lord's, the starts to the England innings had been poor. It was decided, therefore, to bring in Wayne for Graham Gooch at the Oval and to give Paul Parker of

Sussex a match in place of David Gower. In their wisdom the selectors knew that it is always a good idea to change a winning side just in case the players become complacent! The Sixth Test was something of an anti-climax after the excitement of the summer. Wayne featured in an opening partnership of 61 with Geoff Boycott and added 70 with Mike Gatting in the second innings before he was caught by Alderman at second slip off Lillee. Needing 383 to win, England pottered along to 261 for 7 wickets before the match petered out in a draw. Wayne had every reason to feel that this had been a good comeback match for him.

Northants had in the meantime been making excellent progress in the NatWest Trophy – the bank having taken over the sponsorship of the premier one-day competition from Gillette – and had reached their fourth Lord's final in five years. On a bright and clear September morning, doubtless hoping for a little early morning green in the wicket, Barry Wood, the Derbyshire captain, invited Northants to bat and Wayne and Geoff Cook added 99 before Wayne left for 52. His partner went on to an excellent 111, but, sadly, Northants lost the match on the very last ball of the 120 overs bowled, when Derby levelled the scores and won as a result of having lost fewer wickets. Geoff was able to console himself with the man of the match award, but the impact of his century was going to have considerable repercussions on Wayne's life.

On the domestic front, Jane and Wayne were installed in their new home in Hardingstone and on 30 May, Jane gave birth to Philippa Jane, their first child, at Northampton's Maternity Home. It was a shame that Wayne somehow managed to miss

Wayne glances to fine leg. (George Herringshaw: www.sporting-heroes.net)

the birth, as the County had a break in their programme on that day. He must have felt that he was a virtual certainty for England's tour of India beginning in November and the two months after the end of the English season would give him time to adjust to his new form of family life. In early September, in preparation for the County's last match against Yorkshire in Scarborough, the Northants team were practising at Wantage Road and there was some expectation that the side for India would be announced that morning. Sure enough, the Northants media appeared at Wantage Road and, with Julian Baskcomb from The *Chronicle & Echo* at the fore, they came onto the ground and walked towards the nets where Geoff Cook, Wayne and several others were batting and bowling. Wayne walked towards them, but they passed him by and went over to congratulate Geoff on his selection as an opening batsman for the Indian tour. It was somewhat reminiscent of the heavyweight title fight ten years earlier when Joe Bugner had defeated Henry Cooper for the British crown. Henry had walked towards Harry Gibbs, the referee, but was brushed aside and Gibbs raised Bugner's hand. 'I thought I just nicked it, Harry,' Henry said. 'Son,' Gibbs is said to have replied, 'champions don't nick anything.' Wayne was no champion either. He was mortified. 'I wanted someone to dig me a big hole so that I could jump in it', he told the press at the time. He just packed his cricket bag and went home to Jane. She wept, because they both believed that Wayne had finally cleared the barrier into England's ranks. After so many near-misses, this was a bad knock, a huge blow to Wayne's pride. Indeed, many have commented that rejection is something that hurts him more than it does other people.

People, listening on the radio far away from Northamptonshire, thought that they must have misheard the radio announcement. Surely the Cook chosen for the tour must be Nick, Leicestershire's slow left-arm bowler? But no, Geoff Cook was the selectors' choice. He had come to Wantage Road from Middlesbrough with a bunch of young players, including Wayne, in around 1970. The Northants establishment had seen that he had greater leadership abilities than his contemporaries and with the uncertainty surrounding the captaincy at the end of the 1970s they had groomed him for the role, while Jim Watts acted mainly as caretaker in his second stint in the job. Other reasons have been advanced for his inclusion, the most obvious and the one held by most of the Northants players of that time being that his ton in the Lord's final had just 'nicked' it for him over Wayne's half-century. Even the bumblings of England's selectors must have produced a more reasoned conclusion than this and the more likely reason was that they believed that Geoff Cook was England captaincy material and that their choice for the India tour, Keith Fletcher of Essex, was to be a mere stopgap, as, indeed, he proved to be.

Geoff Cook comes out of this affair with flying colours. He has said to this day that he was lucky to be chosen and even felt embarrassed that Wayne had been rejected in favour of him. He never did become England captain, but between 1981 and 1989 he became Northamptonshire's longest-serving county captain, a post which he held with much dignity and some considerable success. Yet, once again, Wayne was out in the wilderness. Had he been selected to go to India in the autumn of 1981 and bat on their flat wickets he would, almost certainly, have cemented a place for himself in England's Test team, but it was not to be. The selectors' decision, a cavalier one in the minds of many people, exerted an enormous effect on the whole of Wayne's life from that point onward.

7
LARKINS MICAWBER

After the intense disappointment of failing to be included on the tour of India and Sri Lanka, Wayne did not really expect his fortunes to change, but he did hope that some door might open. In fact, one did, but only after some months, and it proved to be one of the defining moments of his career. In some respects it was the most important decision that he ever took professionally and it was an unhappy one at that. It was to mean that he would not play another international match for the best part of a decade.

For the present, however, he had to seek work and his qualifications for well-paid employment were minimal. 'The only thing I know anything about and can do well is cricket,' he has said on several occasions, and here he was being denied, as he and many others around Northampton saw it, the chance to practise what he was good at. Feeling sorry for himself is not part of the Larkins make-up nor, sadly, is making the best of himself. A few beers and the packet of Silk Cut seemed largely to be the consolation, although he did enjoy a quick trip to Wellkom in the Orange Free State in October 1981. Partnered by Peter Willey, he went off to play in a double wicket competition, in which England colleagues Mike Hendrick, Chris Old and Geoff Miller were all involved. Wiser heads like the New Zealanders John Wright and Richard Hadlee kept their distance. Allan Lamb was also playing and this was to have a certain ironic significance in the following year. There was a mini storm as a result of pressure from African and Asian nations about England players performing in South Africa, although it has to be said that enough of them had been coaching in that country for a number of years. Wayne was quite adamant that he was doing the right thing and told the press: 'I am a professional cricketer. I've got to earn a living like everyone else and it is possible that means playing in the winter.' As things panned out, the Lord's authorities did not feel under sufficient pressure to take any action.

Wayne was able to enjoy the pleasures of fatherhood, but a wife who had given up work and a new daughter brought financial pressures which were a considerable strain. Jane had enjoyed the limelight of being married to a man who was well-known and, in the world of cricket if not in the workrooms of the British Shoe Corporation, highly respected and liked. It is clearly not everyone's husband who appears regularly throughout the summer on the sports pages of the national dailies, and their home and lifestyle in Hardingstone would not have been possible without Wayne's cricketing prowess. In November the India tour party left for the sub-continent. Chris Tavaré, who had been recalled to the England ranks along with David Gower at the expense of Wayne and Paul Parker in this sad game of selectorial musical chairs, has described Wayne's omission as the 'key point' in his career. Chris is a modest and thoughtful man, an Oxford graduate, a captain of both Kent and Somerset and now a biology teacher in his old school at Sevenoaks. He knew that he owed his selection to the fact that he could, in his own words, 'hang around' while the stroke-makers like Gower, Gatting and Botham could make hay at the other end. While a series against India on their own pitches is never less than a total fight against

Wayne batting for Northamptonshire in 1981. (Bill Smith)

outstandingly fluent batsmen and world-class spinners, it does give batsmen from abroad the chance to play on some very flat pitches indeed. It is almost inconceivable that Wayne would not have scored stacks of runs in India, and England's top order did precisely that. Eight batsmen, including Geoff Cook, Chris Tavaré and second wicketkeeper Jack Richards, had averages in excess of 40 for the first-class matches and a ninth, Mike Gatting, was only one run behind.

In spite of all this, however, it was not a particularly happy tour. The First Test against India was lost, the next five drawn and England ended up 2-1 down in the one-day internationals. Keith Fletcher, the England captain, a man noted for his common sense and sportsmanship, managed to blot his copybook in the Second Test at Bangalore when he knocked off a bail with his bat after being dubiously given out caught at the wicket. For a skipper who had been telling his team to accept the Indian umpiring, it was an unworthy reaction and he had to write a note of apology to the Indian Board. After India, the England party moved down to Sri Lanka, shared the one-dayers, one apiece, and won the inaugural Test between the two countries, in which Geoff Cook made his Test debut, by seven wickets.

Something else was stirring too. As long ago as February 1981, almost a year previously, Geoff Boycott had been seen at the team's Hilton Hotel at Port-of-Spain, Trinidad, in deep conversation with a South African businessman by the name of Peter Cooke. A week or two later, the team were in the Pegasus Hotel in Georgetown, Guyana, awaiting what proved to be unfruitful negotiations on the selection for the England team of Robin Jackman, the Surrey bowler whose South African links had upset the Guyana government. Boycott decided to call a number of senior players together. It transpired that Peter Cooke was sounding out the English players about the possibility of an England tour to South Africa, where the country's sporting isolation, owing to the *apartheid* policy, was beginning to hurt. The Holiday Inn hotel chain was the potential backer and vast sums of money were being talked about. No firm commitments were made and the summer defeat of the Australians came and went, before another meeting was called at the Holiday Inn in Kensington just prior to the Indian touring party's departure. Some of the players invited to the discussions began to take a real interest in the South African proposals, despite a TCCB letter to all contracted county cricketers warning them of the Gleneagles agreement. This undertaking had been signed at a meeting of Commonwealth Presidents and Prime Ministers in 1977 and was concerned, as part of the campaign against *apartheid,* with discouraging sporting links with South Africa. Cricketers were warned of the problems that might arise if they disregarded it and the two Geoffs, Boycott and Cook, who had spent some time playing and coaching in South Africa in previous winters and had been on a United Nations blacklist, had been forced to make statements of opposition to *apartheid* before they were even allowed to take part in the Indian tour.

The Indian tour had barely begun when a further meeting, run this time by another South African entrepreneur, Peter Venison, was arranged at the Taj Mahal Hotel in Bombay, a massive building which was ideally suited to the holding of clandestine talks. Seven players, Geoff Boycott, Graham Gooch, David Gower, Bob Willis, John Emburey, Ian Botham and Graham Dilley, were invited to attend. Figures up to £50,000 per player for a month's tour in March 1982, were mentioned, although only top dogs were likely to receive the maximum sum. This sort of negotiation rumbled on for much of the tour, which certainly gave rise later to suggestions of double-dealing, even 'treachery'. Keith Fletcher, the skipper, remained blissfully unaware, while Raman Subba Row, the manager, began to suspect something, but was unable to get at the truth. At this stage, David Gower, who had many friends in the West Indies, and Ian Botham, who said that he would have never been able to look his Somerset friend and colleague, Viv Richards, in the face again if he accepted, dropped out, but the others apparently remained hooked. The number of players from the touring party now included Derek Underwood and John Lever, but those who were really interested were insufficient to make up a South African touring team and other players had to be approached. At this point Wayne became involved and soon learned that Alan Knott, Peter Willey, Mike Hendrick and Chris Old, all of whom had missed the Indian tour and were enjoying the English winter climate, were now taking the bait. In the end they were joined by Dennis Amiss, Geoff Humpage, Les Taylor, Bob Woolmer and, rather late on, by Arnie Sidebottom.

The South African Breweries 'Rebel' tour, in March 1982. From left to right, back row: Wayne Larkins, Bob Woolmer, liaison officer, Les Taylor, Chris Old, Mike Hendrick, Peter Willey, John Lever. Front row: Geoff Humpage, Derek Underwood, Geoff Boycott, Graham Gooch (captain), Peter Cooke (liaison officer), Dennis Amiss, Alan Knott. (Bob Thomas)

No sooner had the touring party got back to England than all those who had taken the blood money soon found themselves flying out to Johannesburg. Some, like Derek Underwood, John Lever and even Peter Willey, wrongly as it happens, may have felt that their England careers were drawing to a close, others like Graham Gooch and John Emburey felt they were professional cricketers and entitled to earn money where they could, while Les Taylor of Leicestershire, who was already coaching in South Africa, had always felt that his miner's background counted against him when teams were selected in the posh surroundings of Lord's. He may have had a point. But Wayne was the only one who, while not discounting the financial rewards, really went out of pique. Even many years later it still rankles with him that nobody from amongst England's selectors had sought to explain to him why he had been omitted from the India tour party.

The tour of March 1982, now sponsored by South African Breweries, as Holiday Inns had backed out, was no big deal in cricketing terms, despite the large amounts of money floating about. The organisers had really failed in their prime objective when Ian Botham, who was offered a 'name your price' contract, refused to be drawn into the tour. Despite being the main mover in the affair and not normally a wallflower in the captaincy stakes, Geoff Boycott did not wish to take the lead on the field, and the task went to a thoroughly unprepared Graham Gooch, who had had very little experience of captaincy. There were three one-day games against a side styled as 'South Africa' containing such eminent players as Barry Richards, Graeme Pollock, Clive Rice and Mike Proctor, all of whom had been denied their rightful number of international appearances because of their country's isolation.

All three one-day matches were won by the South Africans, and there were also three four-day 'Tests,' which the hosts shaded by 1-0 with two draws. Graham Gooch scored a couple of tons, Bob Woolmer one and Wayne turned in an excellent 95 in the second 'Test'. They all came back feeling pretty well remunerated for a month's work and Wayne, while not among the highest paid, had £20,000 in his pocket to help pay off his mortgage on the Hardingstone house. But the real fun had already begun back home.

The Prime Minister, Margaret Thatcher, was said to be 'dismayed' at the news of the tour and the Sports Minister, Neil McFarlane, accused the team of 'deception'. The press, presumably because of technical difficulties with their abacus, named the fifteen players the 'dirty dozen.' Labour MP Gerald Kaufman, in a speech full of emotion, said, 'They are selling themselves for blood-covered Krugerrands,' while Michael Foot, the Labour Leader and David Steel of the Liberals joined in with criticism in that general uproar which is Prime Minister's question time in the House of Commons. The cricket authorities also expressed an opposition, the vehemence of which surprised many of the 'rebel' team. For Peter Willey and Wayne, things were even worse. Ken Turner, the

Wayne, watched by John Lever, shows his footballing skills as he fields in the Second 'Rebel' Test versus South Africa. (Bob Thomas)

Northants secretary, went ballistic when he heard the news. 'It's a bloody conspiracy. I have nothing but contempt for all of them,' he fumed to the local press. 'They have given no thought to anyone else in the game but themselves and are political pawns who have succumbed to avarice.'

The TCCB was asked to consider action against all those involved in the tour, particularly as the Indian and Pakistani Cricket Boards had chimed in with threats that they would pull out of the summer tours if any of the 'rebel' players were chosen for England. The Northants cricket committee put forward a resolution that all those involved in the SAB tour should have their county registrations cancelled. The Board needed to be very careful on this point because 'restraint of trade' had been a central plank of the players' case at the time of the Packer Affair, and it became clear then that, while an established county player had no inalienable right to be selected for his country – after all, the selectors managed a pretty fair old game of moving chessmen on a board without any other help – he could not be easily removed from his county side if he has been a regular member of it for some time. This move was defeated, but all those involved in the tour received a ban from Test cricket for three years. For some whose Test careers were nearing the end this was no real problem, but Wayne was not yet twenty-nine years of age and the early 1980s could well have been the time when his career as a Test batsman might have flourished.

The players were flabbergasted at the length of the ban. They had thought that a year would be the maximum time, but they had, to an extent, misread the feelings of most ordinary county cricketers. While they received support from Tory backbencher John Carlisle, who tabled a motion congratulating the players on going to South Africa, and from the die-hard Tory MPs from Northampton, Michael Morris and Tony Marlowe ('Every freeborn Englishman is free to carry out his business wherever he wishes' was the latter's contribution to the debate), the Annual General Meeting of the Professional Cricketers' Association which met in April at Edgbaston voted 190 to 35 to support the TCCB ban. Although the majority of those present were unlikely to be England cricketers, they recognised that they depended to a great extent on the profits from international matches. If England, so they argued, found that it could play Test cricket merely in a microcosm with Australia, South Africa and New Zealand, their own pockets would be affected.

Much is talked about sport and politics. Some will always say that they are separate issues and should remain so, but wiser minds need to reflect on the impact of cricketers failing to take account of the wider issues. Jim Watts, Northants' former captain and usually a good friend to Wayne, was angry with him. 'The sooner we get rid of players who do not support the interests of their fellow cricketers in the game in general, then the better it will be for the clubs,' he commented to the *Chronicle & Echo* in Northampton. He was, of course, foreseeing some of the problems that might occur not only at international level but also nearer home at county level if, for instance, the Pakistani and Indian authorities pronounced that players such as Kapil Dev or Sarfraz Nawaz might not play alongside 'rebel' players in the same county side. Fortunately, this situation did not occur, but a coach and horses might have been driven through the overall arrangements for county cricket and it would have been very much to the detriment of the ordinary contracted player.

Jim Swanton, the respected cricket journalist, probably summed up what the majority of English people thought:

So far as cricket is concerned, the issue is clear. Do we abide by the spirit of the Gleneagles Agreement and respect the convictions of our own Government and the Commonwealth, and thus preserve both Test cricket and county cricket on which it is entirely dependent? Or do we allow the whole vulnerable fabric of the English game built up over a century or more to disintegrate before our eyes? This is the question South African sympathisers must answer.

Wayne was forced to accept the situation, but was aggrieved. He had always felt an enormous pride when he had been picked for England and must have found it hard to fathom how Zola Budd from South Africa was cavorting around with the English Olympic Team and, on a more personal level, how Allan Lamb, his Northants colleague, was about to step into the England team in the 1982 Tests against Pakistan and India when he had spent much of his life and played much of his cricket in South Africa. Allan Lamb himself, never to be accused of being a shrinking violet, admitted in his autobiography that he felt a certain embarrassment when he was in the same dressing room as Wayne and Peter Willey, who clearly felt bitter about the situation. In spite of this, however, Wayne and Peter were among the first to congratulate Lamby when he received his call-up to play for England.

8

IT'S A COLD POMP

It is a truism to say that life is unkind, but this is very often the case in the world of professional sport. Peter Willey, Graham Gooch and Wayne, together with other members of the South African Breweries tour party, had sought to have their ban lifted or reduced. The Lord's establishment believed, probably rightly, that they needed to be politically correct if they were to maintain amicable relations with all the Test match-playing nations and they did not wish England's Test opponents to be restricted to just Australia, South Africa and New Zealand. The 'rebels', therefore, had to return to their counties and play their best there. It was a small mercy perhaps, but at least they had not been banned from county cricket, a scenario that had been in the air at the outset.

At the start of the 1982 season, Wayne's first as a banned Test player, he was not yet twenty-nine years of age. It is perhaps ironic that over the course of the next four seasons, he showed an amazing run of form. Was it because he was under no pressure to vault over the bar into the world of Test cricket where he had displayed his familiar problem with adapting to a new environment? Was it, perhaps, because he was just coming good as a fully mature batsman? Was he perhaps determined to show the establishment what he thought of them for banning him? It is impossible to know for sure, but it is true is that Wayne constantly told the press that he was determined to win back an England place, yet at the same time he showed a certain self-conscious defiance towards authority by sporting his South African Breweries blazer rather too often up and down the county grounds.

In the four seasons 1982-85 Wayne scored nearly 7,000 runs, mainly for Northants, with sixteen tons, two of them past the 200 mark. In the same period only four players, who in fact had 355 Test caps between them at the end of their careers, Graham Gooch, Dennis Amiss, Geoff Boycott and Mike Gatting, in any way competed with Wayne, while those who tended to open the innings for England at this time, mainly Chris Tavaré, Graeme Fowler, Chris Broad, Chris Smith and Geoff Cook, were way behind in the runs stakes. Wayne, it must be remembered, ended his career with a paltry thirteen Test caps.

Northamptonshire's 1981 season, Geoff Cook's first as skipper, had not been a resounding success. Fifteenth place in the County Championship, bottom in the Sunday League and a marked lack of success in the one-day competitions, except the loss to Derbyshire in the final of the Natwest Trophy, were hardly the basis of a great record. In addition to all this, there was also tension in the air at Wantage Road in the early summer of 1982 as a result of the County's anger at Wayne and Peter Willey's 'treachery'. Ken Turner, however, did a *volte-face* and said to the press: 'This club has at no stage considered taking unilateral action against their own players. We shall stand by the decision of the TCCB.' This was a far less harsh attitude from the one expressed a few weeks earlier! Geoff Cook had seen it as a sad episode for the English game, and had turned down the offer to take part himself (less than charitable voices thought that he saw an England opener's job on the horizon), but he was determined to put the matter behind him and ask the whole team to get on with the new season.

Northants started their 1982 Championship season with a string of seven draws and

Northants players enjoy the fun of a commercial presentation. From left to right, back row: Wayne Larkins, Jim Griffiths, George Sharp, Tim Lamb. Middle row: David Steele, Mike Bamber, Richard Williams, Allan Lamb. Front row: Geoff Cook, Rob Bailey, Peter Willey.

two losses before they beat Gloucestershire in mid-July. They had two overseas players at different times in the side, Sarfraz Nawaz from Pakistan in the first part of the season and the great Indian all-rounder, Kapil Dev, in the second. Appearing in the same side as Wayne and Peter apparently did not cause the rumpus that had been forecasted. The Famous Five were at the top of the order, although Allan Lamb was often away playing for England, while the bowling was well-balanced with both pace and spin.

In the opening match against Yorkshire at Wantage Road, where Geoff Boycott ground out a well-crafted 138 in the visitors' first innings, Wayne carried his bat for 118 out of 223 when it was the County's turn to bat. 'He was beaten often outside the off-stump and there were only occasional glimpses of Larkins displaying his vibrant attacking gifts,' the *Chronicle & Echo* reporter wrote. 'He showed resilience and grim determination few people realised he possessed in such depth as he tamed the Tykes.' After a second Yorkshire declaration Northants were set 335 to win, but in the end they reached a mere 160 for 4 wickets. But this was not before Wayne had hit 10 fours in a blistering innings of 59 that, unfortunately, was not matched by his colleagues.

At the beginning of June, when the County was due to play the Indian touring team, Wayne was saddened to learn that he and Peter Willey were 'unacceptable' to the tourists on account of the South African tour and, as he went out to bat against Nottinghamshire, he was called a 'racist pig' by one spectator. This sort of thing hurt Wayne's essentially simplistic view of life. 'I have no regrets about going to South Africa, although I am disappointed that I can't be selected for England at the moment,' he told the press ingenuously. 'I went to earn my living rather than existing on the dole and they made it worthwhile. It was my own decision, but I didn't set out to go against the TCCB, my county or anyone else.'

Soon afterwards Wayne scored another hundred, this time 137 with 5 sixes and 14 fours against Somerset. The most powerful innings of Wayne's season, however, came in the next match when the County went up to Middlesbrough to play Yorkshire for the second time that season. Julian Baskcomb, writing in the *Chronicle & Echo*, described the match:

> At twenty-nine, Wayne Larkins is batting better than ever before. The tragedy is that the rich run of this world-class natural talent is now restricted to balmy afternoons in far flung places like Middlesbrough rather than the international Test arenas. It was his second century in a week and, if he had only not hastily sacrificed his Test future for bruised pride and the enticing lure of easy money, Larkins would probably be walking out at Old Trafford this week to open the batting with Geoff Cook against India. The Cook and Larkins opening partnership is arguably the best in the country with Cook's sure touch the perfect foil to his partner's flair and aggressive instinct. It is precisely what England are seeking at present, and how well they would have complemented each other at the top level. Sadly, it may never be and this, plus the ban, is something which deeply hurts the sensitive Larkins, who felt that he was doing nothing wrong by going to South Africa. His 186 on a pitch which was always seaming about after three hours delay for rain was quite simply brilliant. Statistics are often misleading, but in the grey murky day they told the whole story of Larkins' path of destruction after Chris Old had decided as captain in his home town to ask Northants to bat first. The driving and leg-side strokes were all irresistible. Larkins reached 50 with a six off Sidebottom and scored his second century against Yorkshire this season in just 114 minutes with a four off Old. As Cook gently reached a two and a half hour century, Larkins' innings, brimming with all the vibrancy of vintage champagne, was closing in on 150, which was reached with yet another boundary in just 165 minutes. Only a handful of batsmen are Larkins' equal in this mood, as Yorkshire's increasingly dispirited and wayward bowlers were chipped with cheeky confidence over the inner ring of fielders. If an attack could appeal against the light they would have gone off. Larkins' surge kept the new £14,000 scoreboard clocking merrily round and he soon went past Raman Subba Row's 158, the best individual score by a Northants batsman against Yorkshire set in 1959, and past his career best 170 against Worcestershire four years ago. He gave just one chance to Athey at slip on 84 and, when he was caught behind off Hartley 102 runs later, he had taken just 61 overs. had batted for 203 minutes and hit 120 in boundaries. The pair added 278 for the first wicket and turned a grey afternoon into a full day's work of vastly entertaining cricket.

Geoff Cook, playing the tortoise to the Larkins hare at the other end and reaching 112 not out, could not have been more impressed. 'In that mood Wayne had virtually no equal as a batsman in the game of cricket. The only person you could compare him with on that murky June afternoon was Viv Richards in full flow.' If Wayne had enjoyed himself, Chris Old, who had put Northants in to bat, had not done so. He had been appointed to the

Yorkshire captaincy in 1981 but on this day, when Wayne ravaged the Yorkshire attack, he found himself peremptorily sacked by Raymond Illingworth, the Yorkshire manager. Ray had never achieved the captaincy of his native county in his serious playing days and had needed to go off to Leicestershire to reach this goal, from which, of course, he had graduated quite quickly to the England post in 1969. He now put matters right and appointed himself captain of Yorkshire, staying in the post until the end of the 1983 season when he was by then fifty-one years old.

In such a rich vein of form, Wayne continued to savage attacks in the County Championship and scored further hundreds against Worcestershire and Derbyshire and an incredibly skilful 81 against Sussex at Eastbourne in August. On a pitch described by Peter Willey as a 'dirt road', he hit 3 towering sixes and 11 fours and this innings, combined with an excellent 103 by Kapil Dev, led the County to an innings victory over the hosts, who were totally unable to cope on their own poorly prepared strip. Three further wins took the County to an improved ninth place at the end of the season. Wayne had been central to their success and his season had produced over 1,800 runs and five tons.

It was not only in the first-class game that Northants made progress in 1982. Their Natwest Trophy form was poor and the Benson & Hedges competition did not produce many good results, although Wayne picked up Gold Awards for his 126 against Scotland and his 132 against Warwickshire. In the John Player League, however, they moved from bottom in 1981 to eighth place. One win was recorded against Worcestershire in August and is beautifully described by Julian Baskcomb in the *Chronicle & Echo* report:

Wayne receives his Gold Award after scoring 126 against Scotland in the Benson & Hedges Cup tie, May 1982.

Wayne Larkins played one of the biggest and most spectacular innings in the history of Sunday League cricket against Worcestershire at Luton's aptly named Wardown Park. He wreaked two hours of magnificent mayhem and finished with 158, just five runs short of the best individual score held by Gordon Greenidge. Numerous records were left sprawling in the wake of an extraordinary third wicket onslaught with Richard Williams that put Northants in a virtually unassailable position. It all started rather inconspicuously as the County took thirteen overs to limp to 37 for two wickets. I daresay a few would have given a penny for Patel's thoughts later in the innings. He dropped Larkins in the deep with his score on eight. The appearance of change-bowler, Steve Perryman, gave the opener the taste for destruction and, as successive sixes vanished into the privet hedge at square-leg, the fuse was ignited. Suddenly there was no looking back and the ball was relentlessly harvested with expert placement, making a mockery of five helpless fielders back on the ropes. The 100 stand took a paltry thirteen overs, while Larkins smashed everything in sight, including the pavilion window, with a fifth sixth to reach an 86 minute century in shattering style. Williams' splendid supporting role was inevitably overshadowed as the unstoppable Larkins proved that he was capable of equalling anything that Garfield could care to dish out as he crashed a sixth six. The blow brought up the 200 and also made Larkins the top individual scorer for Northants, beating Allan Lamb's 127 against the same county last year. With five overs remaining even more risks were taken, and on 132 Larkins was missed on the mid-wicket boundary by Mark Scott, the ball trickling over for four more and setting a new John Player League record for the third wicket. The thrills continued as Larkins passed 150 but, with three overs left and in a stand worth a massive 215, the opener got a top edge to end a magnificent innings which had lasted just 123 minutes and included 6 sixes and a dozen fours. Larkins' career best was unforgettable, not because of the number of runs, but the manner in which he made them.

Few, if any, English batsmen in the early 1980s could produce such blistering form. Wayne was, however, becoming something of a Jekyll and Hyde character. On the field, his batting showed determination and flair and it looked an art in the flow of his strokes. David Capel talks of his batting as oozing ability, quality and style, and goes on: 'Although he was a very quick scorer, Ned never really slogged the ball. If you were to compare him with Geoff Boycott, you could say that Boycott was able to play as many shots as he wanted to, as was the case with Ned. If you look at it the other way round, Ned could certainly have defended quite as well as Boycott.' Off the field, however, it could be another story. While Wayne was never unkind or malicious, he could be careless, forgetful, a dreadful timekeeper and sometimes drove his wife to despair with his eccentric behaviour. At one point she even banned him from having a front door key to their home as he was constantly losing them. His hard drinking, a habit which can be endemic in cricket pavilions, was also a cause for concern in some quarters. Yet it is fair to say that it was rare that he was unfit to play in a match on the following morning. Some say that his evening drinking was his way of winding down from the exertions of the day and ensuring a good night's sleep. And there can be no doubt that he was beginning to think hard about the game. Tim Lamb recalls vividly how he would often see Wayne sitting in the dressing room at Wantage Road by the sliding glass doors at the end of a day's play, a pint of lager in his hand and maybe a cigarette, just unwinding. 'He did not do this in any kind of unsociable way; it wasn't as if he were in a tunnel and not trying to contribute because he would engage in any banter or conversation that was going on, but it was his way of thinking about the day that had gone past and, apart from anything else, it was a measure of his commitment to the game. He was still thinking actively after the day was over.' All his colleagues recognised that he was fiercely committed to the team and its corporate well-being. It is clear that, like all batsmen, he took great pleasure in good personal performance, but he was always a really fine team member and, unlike many outstanding batsmen, the eye he cast at the scoreboard was not at his own score, but at that of the team. This has contributed to his constant popularity with the men of his profession.

Most clouds have a silver lining and Wayne's foray to South Africa earlier in the year brought an unexpected benefit to his life in the winter months. Working in the shoe room at the British Shoe Corporation in Northampton or as a gas distiller with Greene King Breweries at Biggleswade had never been much fun and now he perhaps began to see it as below what he wanted for himself. As luck would have it, when he was on the 'rebel' tour he had been able to negotiate a contract to play for Eastern Province in the Currie Cup and, after the end of the English season in October 1982, Wayne, Jane and the eighteen-month old Philippa were able to fly to Port Elizabeth and take up residence in the La Rochelle apartments until April in the following year. Compared with many of Wayne's winters, this was one of comfort, even opulence. The beaches were marvellous for the family and Wayne, a proficient golfer, enjoyed the fine South African courses.

Wayne graced St George's Park, Port Elizabeth, and some of the other attractive South African grounds in the 1982/83 southern season. Graham Gooch, who had signed on at Cape Town for Western Province, had a more prolific season with them than either Wayne or Peter Willey could manage in their seven games for Eastern Province, but for Wayne it proved a happy period in his life and his coaching of younger players, such as James Carse and David Richardson, and the beneficial effect that he exerted on their game proved pleasurable and rewarding to both parties. Furthermore, Lord's seemed to accept that, while the players were banned from Test cricket, they could spend their winters in whatever country they pleased.

Before the new season began, Wayne and Peter Willey were involved in an industrial tribunal, which was the result of the County's sacking of their groundsman, Les Bentley, who had replaced the former Northants player, Albert Lightfoot, in 1977. Les Bentley was a cheerful fellow from Yorkshire, who displayed at times a lack of flexibility. He was, for instance, unwilling to allow the old Northants tradition to continue that allowed children play on the outfield during the intervals. He also did not like people interfering with his job and, probably because of this, he came into conflict with the Secretary, Ken Turner, who was generally used to having his own way in matters concerning the County. The pitches had previously not been good, but Bentley effected some improvement and the whole of Wantage Road looked, in Wayne's words, 'as pretty as a picture.' Ken Turner decided by June 1982, however, that Bentley had to go and, when in August the wicket for the Under 19 Test of England versus the West Indies was such that the game finished in two days, Lord's were furious and Bentley received his P45 from the County. Turner then brought back a friend of his, Norman Hever, the former Glamorgan opening bowler, who had undertaken a previous stint in the post before going to work for a seed company. The Committee, with one exception, supported Turner. Jim Watts, the former skipper, felt that Bentley had had a raw deal. The groundsman, therefore, decided to follow the Bedi path and take the club to an industrial tribunal. Jim Watts resigned from the Committee and spoke on his behalf. Wayne and Les Bentley had often had more than one beer after the game and both he and Peter Willey were asked to attend the tribunal. Turner had

Wayne flaunts his 'Rebel Tour' blazer in England.

triumphed in the fight with Bedi, and on this occasion he won what some wag rather dramatically called the Second Battle of Bedford. Wayne and Peter, who had been sporting their South African tour blazers, were hauled before the Committee and asked to explain themselves. Wayne was apologetic and promised his allegiance, but Peter, the Clint Eastwood of a *Cricketer* magazine article at that time, was never a push-over and was not prepared to give any assurances. He fired his six-shooter firmly at the Committee. Quite predictably, when he was offered nothing more than a one-year contract at the end of the season, he promptly signed for Leicestershire. It was a sad situation, made all the more poignant by the fact that Peter had been named the County's Player of the Year for the second time in succession. The era of the Famous Five was over; in the course of the years it had had a touch of infamy too.

If 1982 had been a marvellous season for Wayne, 1983 proved to be just as good. In the early part of the summer the County drew five Championship games on the trot and Wayne's form was merely adequate, mainly as the result of his having sustained three separate finger injuries on the same hand. But it was not an augury of what was to come later. Prior to Wayne's run glut, however, something else happened. The night before the Surrey match at the Oval, he had attended a dinner for former England players and arrived at the ground on the following morning somewhat the worse for wear. After the net practice some of the players queried with Geoff Cook whether Wayne was fit to play. His legendary powers of recovery from the happenings of the previous night apparently came to his rescue – at least, in so far as he was selected for the team. Geoff and Wayne opened the innings and the County was soon 3 for 1, Wayne being trapped lbw by David Thomas for just 2. Back in the dressing room, still in his pads, he collapsed on a bench and slept for a good hour before waking up and discovering that his left foot was causing him pain, something that he found extremely puzzling. It provoked great amusement among his colleagues when they revealed to him that he had been to the wicket already and been adjudged lbw!

In July, Northants went across to their neighbours at Derby. The Derby wicket is not known to be particularly friendly to batsmen and Kim Barnett, the home skipper, decided to give Northants first knock. Geoff Cook and Peter Willey went quite early, but then Robin Boyd-Moss joined Wayne in a partnership worth 211 for the third wicket before the former fell for a well made 80. Assisted further by Richard Williams, Wayne went on to reach his double hundred. Peter Willey and David Steele were sitting in the pavilion when Wayne came into the 220s and then slipped past Peter's 227 which he had made against Somerset in 1976, an occasion when Wayne's poor backing-up had caused Peter to be run out on a day he had fancied himself for 300. Throwing his cap on the ground in mock irritation at the miscreant's success, Peter got up, turned away and disappeared into the pavilion. Wayne's magnificent 236 out of 439 for four wickets declared – a record total against Derbyshire – came to an end just before the declaration. It had taken just 330 minutes and included 2 sixes and 31 fours.

July gave way to August, and towards the end of the month there began a purple patch of batting that was certainly as good as anything that Wayne ever achieved and many a batsman would have liked to do half as well. Against Lancashire at Wantage Road he

The Northamptonshire XI in May 1983. From left to right, back row: Richard Williams, Kapil Dev, Peter Willey, Jim Griffiths, Tim Lamb, Neil Mallender, David Capel. Front row: Allan Lamb, Wayne Larkins, Geoff Cook (captain), George Sharp. (Bob Thomas)

NORTHAMPTON v. GLAMORGAN at on 31, 1 & 2. SEPT. '83

Umpires D. CONSTANT, K. IBADULLA — Scorers A.K. HIGNELL, B.H. CLARKE — Toss won by GLAMORGAN

1st Innings of NORTHANTS (CHOSE TO FIELD)

In	Out	No	Batsman		50 150 / 150 200	How Out	Bowler	
11.00	11.27	1	G. COOK *	4113/2122/		BOWLED	DAVIS	18
11.00	4.58	2	W. LARKINS	3/14114442/343344311/21411113411141242113143141 11211611112312141421314111124123211111121324111144124144	56 183 234 / 129 255 298	C. BARWICK	ROWE	252
11.28	12.12	3	P. WILLEY	21143/		C. FRANCIS	BARWICK	13
12.13	3.06	4	A.J. LAMB	1144142261423424111143114144116144421121424213	51 / 106	C. ONTONG	DAVIS	119
3.07	3.44	5	R.G. WILLIAMS	3/212212142/		C. DAVIES	ONTONG	20
3.45	5.00	6	R.J. BOYD-MOSS	111124122221112		C. DAVIES	ROWE	21
4.59	5.23	7	D.S. STEELE	1411/		C. HOPKINS	WILKINS	7
5.01	5.14	8	G. SHARP	44122/		LBW	ROWE	13
5.15	(5.47)	9	N.A. MALLENDER	2334131		NOT	OUT	17
5.24	(5.47)	10	CARSE. J.	12/224112		NOT	OUT	16
		11	B.J. GRIFFITHS	D.N.B.				

Byes ( ) — L.Byes 4/2 (7) — Wides ( ) — No Balls (26) **33**

Total **529**

	1	2	3	4	5	6	7	8	9	10	
Fall of Wicket	46	106	242 313m 348	396	472	474	494	498			FOR 8 WKTS DEC.
Batsman Out	1	3	4	5	2	6	8	7			
Not Out	2	2	2	2	6	7	7	9			

BOWLING ANALYSIS

Bowler												O	M	R	W	w nb
DAVIS. W.W.												17	1	93	2	
WILKINS. A.H.												16	3	90	1	
BARWICK. S.												11	1	77	. 1	
ROWE. C.J.												23	0	123	3	
ONTONG. R.												23	0	113	1	

REMARKS

LUNCH — 210 FOR 2 WKTS
TEA — 423 " 4 "

TOTAL **90 5 496 8**

RESULT MATCH ABAND'D

Northampton v. Glamorgan, 31 August and 1 and 2 September 1983. This (252) was Wayne's highest score in first-class cricket.

NORTHAMPTON v. *DERBYSHIRE* at *DERBY* on *16. 17. 18. JULY '83*

Umpires *C. COOK / A.G. WHITEHEAD* Scorers *B. W. TACEY / B. H. CLARKE* Toss won by *DERBY.*

1st Innings of *NORTHANTS.* (*CHOSE TO FIELD*)

In	Out	Nº	Batsman		50 150 / 150 200	How Out	Bowler	
11.00	11.20	1	COOK. G. ✱	141		C. ANDERSON	OLDHAM.	6
11.00	5.30	2	LARKINS. W.	124 111 64 1164 1142 1142 1 3434 2424 1143 2444 444 1144 1143 12 1461 1 / 1111 44 1341 4 11111 242 111 4 1122 31417 2 42 111 22111 2114 633 22 11 / 112 1111141	123 237 / 166 3/0	BOWLED	FOWLER	236
11.21	12.39	3	WILLEY. P.	12 1111 1141	1 41144		C. MOIR	MORTENSEN	15
12.40	3.48	4	BOYD-MOSS. R.J.	1144 2144 144 1414 224 42 11444 111 4A41 /	102	BOWLED	MOIR	80
3.49	(5.41)	5	WILLIAMS. R.G.	44 14444224 2244 42 1211 134434 111 31212	71	NOT	OUT	73
5.31	(5.41)	6	KAPIL DEV.	2411113		NOT	OUT	13
		7	STEELE. D.S					
		8	SHARP. G.					
		9	LAMB. T.M.	*DID NOT BAT*				
		10	WALKER. A.					
		11	GRIFFITHS. B.J					

Byes *1* (*1*) L.Byes *111-3-3-1* (*10*) Wides *111.* (*3*) No Balls *11* (*2*) 16

	1	2	3	4	5	6	7	8	9	10	Total	439
Fall of Wicket	13	62	273	414								
Batsman Out	1	3	4	2							FOR 4 WKTS	
Not Out	2	2	2	5							DECL.	

BOWLING ANALYSIS

Bowler	1	2	3	4	5	6	7	8	9	10	O	M	R	W	w nb
MORTENSON. O.	1 –M– 3...4.⁴ 30.4..3.³⁷	51...⁵ 521..2.⁴⁰	7.1.+.⁷ 541.4..⁴⁵	181...⁸ 51213.·5²	20...4.¹² 58.41.14⁶²	22..11...¹⁴ 601.4.4⁷¹	74.4..21	26..W~|²²	28...44.³⁰		16	1	71	1	1
OLDHAM. S.	21..1..² 36..1..²⁷ 50.24..2³⁶	42..4.⁵ 28.3.4²⁴ 82.1.2.9¹	6.. HH 40.414..⁴³ 841..4.⁷⁶	8.. –M– 42 40.4.1.⁵²	16.11...¹⁰ 44 1...⁵³	12.-.11 46 12.1.⁵⁷	1414...¹⁶ 181...¹⁵⁹	16...1..¹⁷ 5c1.42.⁶⁶	524...²¹ 76..4.(3.⁷³	24.14..²⁶ 75.-9..41⁷⁸	23	2	96	1	1
FINNEY. R.	9...1 40..M~	4 1.21..⁴ 68 1....²⁷	13.1...⁴ 70.41..⁵²	15.4.1.¹⁰ 72-4.41⁴¹	17. –M– 74 –M–	19.0.4.¹⁵	5|..4.¹⁹	23 –M–	621...¹	141..4.²⁶	15	4	41	0	1 1
WATTS. A.	25. –M–	27+...1¹	29-3...⁴	21..12..⁷	33.2....⁹	35 –M–	37.4..3.¹⁶	39.44....²⁴	41..4.4.³²	43..4.43⁴³	10	2	43	0	1
MOIR. D.	45. –M– 45.242. 55-22.1.⁷⁰	37.461.4.¹⁵ 67.11–N~⁵¹ 87.1-12.⁸⁴	49 –M– 69 1....⁵² 1.9...462⁹⁴	51....¹⁶ 71.2..2.⁵⁶ 91.2..⁹⁷	13.4..²⁰ 73 –M–	554.4..²⁴ 75.4..4⁶⁴	57 –M– 77...1..⁶⁵	59.4...³⁵ 79..-1..⁶⁶	61..11..³⁵ 81..4.⁷⁰	63.1.14.⁴¹ 83.1..4⁷⁵	24	4	97	1	
FOWLER. W.P.	86..14..⁵	28 211..11	90..1..¹²	42 221 431²⁵	94 1144 N¹	96 31-11.⁴²	98 1-13-2⁴⁷				7	0	49	1	
ANDERSON. I.S.	91 33..4¹⁰	93 414...¹⁹	951.2..4.²⁶								3	0	26	0	

REMARKS		
	LUNCH — 98 FOR 2 WKTS.	TOTAL 98 13 423 4
	TEA — 293 + 3 o	
		RESULT *MATCH DRAWN*

Northampton v. Derbyshire, 16, 17, 18 July 1983. Wayne reached 236, his first double hundred.

Wayne, aged twenty-nine, in his record-breaking year of 1983.

joined Peter Willey in a second wicket stand of 342 as they demolished the record Wayne and Richard Williams had set against Leicestershire in 1980. When Wayne went for 187, they were just 35 runs short of the highest ever partnership for the County. Peter was left on 147 not out when Geoff Cook applied the closure at 381 for two wickets. The *Chronicle & Echo* reporter catches the flavour of this magnificent piece of batsmanship from what he termed the 'Pirate Pair.'

> *Larkins has admitted that he is determined to prove his worth as a future England opener during his years in the cold. On Saturday there was no doubt of his class as he stayed at the crease for six hours, starting up cautiously and working up to a splendid exhibition of stroke play, as he went past his 1,000 runs for the season. Few can match Larkins in this mood. He made a mockery of the general verdict among the experts that Test bans have robbed England of only three openers: Geoff Boycott, Graham Gooch and Bob Woolmer. After Larkins had reached his second Championship ton in 256 minutes and Willey his in 232 minutes, the crowd were treated to some effortless scoring on a easy-paced pitch. Landmark followed landmark, none coming more convincingly than when Larkins hit spinner David Lloyd for a straight six to bring up the 300. He hit another six and a four in the same over. The record stand was reached in the 106th over and there was still time for Larkins to greet the new ball with a further six out of the ground off fast-bowling terror Les McFarlane. The cheering of the crowd must have been ringing in Clive Lloyd's ears. Six hours earlier he had decided to field on an overcast morning. In the 109th over Larkins mistimed a pull to mid-on to bring to a close the partnership of the two forgotten men of English cricket.*

This innings was just a curtain-raiser for Wayne. A few days later he took the Glamorgan attack for a masterly 145 and, after a visit to Leicester, the County travelled to Cardiff to play their second match in as many weeks against Glamorgan. Wayne again started demolishing record books. He ran up a career best 252, which took the County to an unbelievable 529 for eight wickets declared in just ninety overs, and bettered his 236 against Derbyshire made six weeks previously. His two great innings, sandwiching Alvin Kallicharran's 243 not out for Warwickshire against Glamorgan, were the top innings in 1983. Allan Lamb, with 119, joined Wayne in an electrifying stand of 242 in 133 minutes in just 36 overs and Wayne's 252 included many a milestone. He reached his ton two overs before lunch, scored another 100 runs between lunch and tea, enjoying nothing other than a few fags and a cup of tea at both intervals. When he was finally caught at deep mid-off after tea, his innings had taken 220 balls, had lasted 298 minutes and had included 28 fours and 1 six. It was also the highest score ever recorded at Sophia Gardens, Cardiff. It was certainly a cause for celebration, and Wayne and Richard Peel, a top reporter at the *Chronicle & Echo* and nowadays ITV's Director of Public Relations, went on the town. 'We drank fifteen pints; I know because I counted them', Richard remembers. 'Between you?' 'Oh no, each of us and when we got back to the hotel I staggered into bed, but Ned popped into the bar for a couple of brandies.'

With what was almost an afterthought, Wayne weighed in with exactly 100 in 143 minutes against Middlesex at Lord's and secured the County a handsome win by seven wickets in an exciting run-chase. It had been a devastating end to the season for Wayne and for Northants. The County had won seven Championship matches and had moved to sixth place in the table. Since going in to bat against Lancashire on 20 August, Wayne had scored 814 runs at an average of 74 and hit 4 hundreds. He ended the season with almost another 1,800 runs and thereby almost emulated his achievements of the previous season. He was, however, still in the doghouse as far as the Committee was concerned. During his winter stay in Port Elizabeth he had played in the same team as James Carse, considered a potentially outstanding fast bowler, and Wayne had recommended him to the County. Carse did not come up to expectations as a bowler and finished with a mere 22 wickets at an average of 33. With the help of eight not out innings out of the ten he played, he finished, ironically, higher in the national averages at the end of the season than anyone except Viv Richards, Gordon Greenidge and Mike Gatting. At this stage Wayne was getting the blame for most things at Wantage Road and the case of Carse, fast bowler manqué, was no exception.

It was not only in the first-class game that Wayne was prominent. Annoyed that he had failed to beat Gordon Greenidge's highest individual score in the Sunday League, when he scored his 158 against Worcestershire in the previous season, he set out again to Wardown Park, Luton, in June with the intention of putting the matter right. And he did just that. Peter Clifton of the *Chronicle & Echo*, with proper aeronautical allusion to Luton airport, describes Wayne's amazing innings:

> *High-flying Wayne Larkins rewrote the record books at Luton yesterday with an unforgettable 172 not out, which sent Northants jetting to victory over Warwickshire with their highest ever total in the Sunday League. It was a day when records went soaring like the aeroplanes overhead. Larkins broke the best individual innings by Gordon Greenidge with an incredible knock, which included 6 sixes and 12 fours, as Northants closed on 298 for two wickets in their forty overs. Previous performances were sent nose-diving as Larkins and Willey, who made 84, put on a jet-powered 234 in 26 overs, the highest ever second wicket partnership in the Sunday League. With fellow*

opener Rob Bailey, Larkins gave the County a solid start and, once his partner had gone, he took command with a string of punishing shots. When the 100 had been raised Larkins signalled what was to come with a 6 over mid-wicket off Norman Gifford, the Warwickshire captain. The latter switched his bowlers in vain as the batting bonanza continued. Larkins' century came in the 32nd over with a boundary off Anton Ferreira and, 2 overs later, the 200 was passed and Willey reached his half-century. Having been dropped on 35 at deep square-leg off Chris Old, Willey really had the crowd fastening their seat-belts as he plundered the 35th over by Willy Hogg for five boundaries. As the excitement reached fever pitch the 250 went up in the 37th over, when Willey had his off-stump sent cartwheeling. With 2 overs to go, Larkins hit Paul Smith for another six, and with the next ball reached 150. A passing jet seemed to dip its wings in salute. From the next ball Larkins was dropped at deep square, but there was still time for him to be caught off a no-ball before he passed the record score with a top-edged four to the fence. The big crowd, which had soaked up plenty of runs and beer, rose to their feet as Larkins celebrated by hitting the next ball from Smith for six and ending the Northants innings.

This had been a truly prodigious innings, although, sadly for Wayne, Graham Gooch pipped his record with an innings of 176 against Glamorgan later in the season. For all that, however, it has remained a Northants record for the best part of two decades. There was another reason why Wayne was lucky that day. It was one of the occasions when BBC Sunday afternoon TV showed some cricket and, although he is not sentimental, Wayne is

Wayne batting at Wardown Park, Luton, in the course of making 172 not out, which at that time was a Sunday League record score. (Bill Smith)

proud to tell people that one of his treasured possessions is the video of his 172.

Wayne had been able to arrange a two-year contract with Eastern Province and in October the Larkins family were able to fly out to Port Elizabeth for a second winter in the sun. In terms of his own batting it was a much greater success than the previous season with tons against Western Province and Natal, 94 against Northern Transvaal and a final average of nearly 50. He did have one chance to play against a 'rebel' West Indian side, but since this team was *persona non grata* with the wider cricket world he declined to take part and met up one day at the Elizabeth Hotel with Mike Green, with whom he had batted long ago for Bedford Second XI in a match in which the fourteen-year-old Wayne's precocious 74 not out had won the day. Mike was in South Africa on a journalistic appointment and together they enjoyed an all-day bender. Jane, even had she wanted to, could not have joined in, as in those unenlightened South African days, most bars were for men only and women were shepherded into a separate room. By the end of the day Mike staggered up to his hotel room and Wayne crawled back to the La Rochelle apartments. On the following morning he rolled up, fresh as a daisy, to drive a thoroughly hung-over Mike to the airport. The latter discovered later that Wayne went off to an afternoon club match and scored a scintillating innings of ninety.

By the standard of the record-breaking achievements of 1982 and 1983, Wayne's next two seasons were modest. In both he scored more runs than any other Northants batsman, although Allan Lamb missed many matches owing to his England commitments. George Sharp, the Northants wicketkeeper and vice-captain of that time, has always said that Lancashire was 'one of Larky's favourite counties' and so it proved at the end of May 1984. Wayne hit a powerful 151 in 274 minutes with 1 six and 17 fours out of a declared total of 378 for 5 wickets. A month later he was called upon to bowl against Warwickshire at Wantage Road and managed to break George Sharp's thumb. George retired hurt and went straight off to Northampton Maternity Home to be present at the birth of his son, Gavin. When he returned to the ground he had to suffer a fair amount of ribbing from his colleagues. How much had he paid Wayne to break his thumb?

Wayne chipped in with an innings of 108 against Somerset in a match which the County lost easily, but the spectators at Wantage Road had to wait until the end of August for another Larkins spectacular. Sussex had batted first and, thanks to 127 from Alan Wells, had reached 391 for 9 wickets declared. Northants lost 4 relatively early wickets, but a fighting 106 not out by Rob Bailey, highly praised by secretary Ken Turner and now finding his feet in the County side, meant that they reached their 300 total and declared 88 runs behind. When Sussex declared, after some further sterling batting by Alan Wells, ably supported by Ian Greig, they had set Northants 303 to win in 65 overs. It proved too generous, although on the face of it 303 looked a hard task on the last day of the match. In the past month Wayne had scored no more than 120 runs before scoring a brisk 86 against Glamorgan in the previous match. But on this day, to quote Peter Clifton of the *Chronicle & Echo*, he 'erupted like a volcano.' Geoff Cook went relatively early, but Wayne then set off to win the match for his side. Peter Clifton takes up the story:

> The signs were good from the start as the free-scoring star cracked three boundaries off paceman Adrian Jones in one over. It was a joy to behold as he produced every shot in the book to leave the Sussex bowling chart like a casualty list after a gangland shoot-out. Good support came from Robin Boyd-Moss, who made 46, and Richard Williams chipped in with a useful 28, but no one looked like shifting Larkins from centre stage

and he cruised to his hundred in 147 minutes with 11 fours and 1 six. With 123 needed off 20 overs there was still a bit to do, but Larkins continued with a dazzling assault on the Sussex bowling. The introduction of South African paceman, Garth Le Roux, in failing light was greeted with a 6 over mid-wicket to reach his 150. The visitors' last round of ammunition had been fired and the County cruised in with a straight six from Rob Bailey. Larkins marched off to a loud reception, finishing with 183 not out including 17 fours and a quartet of sixes. His knock which had lasted only 186 balls was the highest County innings against Sussex, beating Dennis Brookes' 179 in 1948.

This great innings, representing over 60 per cent of the side's total, was wholly typical of Wayne's approach to batting. His team always came first and winning a match was so much more important than making a good score oneself. When it was pointed out to him on one occasion that he had never scored two hundreds in the same match, his response was typical: 'No, I play to win, not to score a hundred every day. I could have done it lots of times if I had tried. That's the difference between people who score 30,000 runs and those who score 20,000 runs in their careers. The former want to get a hundred every time they go out there, no matter what their side needs. I go out to win.' There may be just a little self-delusion in Wayne's comments, but there can never be any doubt about

Wayne, Jane and their daughter, Philippa, in their Hardingstone home in 1984. (John Courtney)

Wayne drives Surrey's Sylvester Clarke in Northamptonshire's match at the Oval in May 1984.

Wayne hooks Surrey fast bowler, David Thomas, in Northamptonshire's match at the Oval, May 1984.

Wayne at Milton Keynes in 1984.

his commitment to winning for his side. Many years later someone said to Wayne: 'I saw you only got 29 the other day.' 'I know, it was a pity I didn't get a few more', he replied, 'but we won, didn't we?'

It was not only with the bat that Wayne was achieving great things. He was captaining the side when Geoff Cook and George Sharp were unavailable and, in the last match of the season at Worcester, he weighed in with 5 wickets for 59 runs off 25 overs of medium pace bowling. Dennis Brookes had believed from the very start of Wayne's career that he had a future as an all-rounder. He was able to swing his medium pace both ways and there is little doubt that he could have made himself into a useful bowler at the highest level in exactly the same way in which Graham Gooch had done. The pleas he often made about a bad back have always seemed a little hollow.

Northants had enjoyed an indifferent season in 1984, dropping back to eleventh in the Championship and reaching the semi-final of the Natwest Trophy was their only significant achievement in the one-day game. Wayne knew that his ban from Test cricket would end in March 1985, and, wisely, he declined to go out to Port Elizabeth for a third winter season. Instead he continued to play some semi-professional soccer to keep the wolf from the door and he also was engaged as a van driver by the Work Force company who provided drivers for other companies when their own staff were unavailable.

The 1985 season was something of 'steady as she goes' for Northamptonshire. They made little upward progress in the Championship and in one-day cricket their best performance was in the Sunday League, where they rose from twelfth to fifth place. It was also a season of steady, but unspectacular progress for Wayne. He scored consistently for the County, but it was not

Wayne bowling for Northants against Middlesex in their match at Uxbridge in July 1985.

Wayne batting for Northants against Middlesex at Uxbridge in July 1985.

until the end of June when the County were facing Surrey at the Oval that he scored his first ton, 117 with 3 sixes and 13 fours out of a winning total of 257 for 5 wickets. This was achieved in 45 overs and was another example of the power of Northants in fourth innings run-chases, when Wayne was at the top of their order. He scored an imposing 140 against Nottinghamshire at Trent Bridge and ended the season with 163 at Worcester, bringing his total runs for the County to just under 1,500 – many more than any Northants batsman.

Wayne had not, of course, been eligible for the 1984/85 winter tour to India and Sri Lanka, and the England side, led by David Gower, had returned in triumph, having won 2-1 in the Test matches against opposition notoriously hard to beat on their home pitches. At the start of the season Wayne had been upbeat about his chances of returning to the England side after his three-year ban. 'I'm looking forward to the new season more than I have done for ages,' he told the press in the early part of the year. 'I really miss the game and I want to get started in the pre-season nets. For the last few years I have played abroad and the County nets in April have hardly filled me with enthusiasm, but now it's a different story.' The Australians arrived in 1985 to contest the Ashes and it seemed unlikely that many changes would be made from the successful Indian touring 'A' party. The openers in possession were Graeme Fowler of Lancashire and Tim Robinson of Nottinghamshire, and Graham Gooch had warned Wayne that the path back to international honours would not be easy. He was, however, determined to regain an England place.

The selectors were only too aware that the Australians were in England and every effort was needed to win. Graeme Fowler was summarily dropped, despite having had a Test average of nearly 55 in India with a top score of 201, and Graham Gooch was recalled, having served his 'rebel' sentence. John Emburey also returned for six Test matches and even Les Taylor and Arnie Sidebottom got a look-in for one Test each. Wayne might perhaps have expected some recognition, but it was not forthcoming. He had scored a solid 44 at Northampton against the touring side which was led by its vice-captain, Andrew Hilditch, his old opening partner from Sutherland days in Sydney, but that was as far as he got.

Wayne also missed out at the end of the season when he failed to make the touring party, which was again led by David Gower, to the West Indies for the 1985/86 winter season. Graham Gooch, John Emburey, Les Taylor and Peter Willey were given the selectors' nod, but Wayne stayed in the wilderness. The selection was flawed from the start as only two openers, Graham Gooch and Tim Robinson, had been chosen, while David Smith, then of Worcestershire, formerly of Surrey and later of Sussex, was considered as a sort of back-up opener, although his experience of the position was virtually nil. The folly of this arrangement was further highlighted when Robinson encountered serious difficulties in facing the West Indian quicks. When Mike Gatting was badly injured by a Malcolm Marshall delivery which struck him in the face, Wilf Slack of Middlesex was flown out as a replacement opener. Wayne was beginning to know that there was little logic in the selectors' deliberations and the fact that he had swept all before him in his years in the wilderness did not seem to count at all. In some respects, of course, it was not a bad tour to miss. England were 'black-washed' in the five Test match series and lost the one-day internationals by 3 to 1. Some changes for the 1986 season seemed to be on the cards. If driving a van and playing soccer for Buckingham Town were scant compensation for Wayne in missing the winter tour, there was one piece of good news for him. The Northants Committee had awarded him a benefit in the 1986 season.

9
FOR WHOSE BENEFIT?

Sportsmen tend to have shorter professional careers than most other people and cricket is no exception. Over the years a system known as the 'benefit' has developed. The Committee normally allocates a particular season to a player of some years' service and the player has to select a match from which he will obtain the takings and, at the same time, arrange dinners, talks, raffles and collections in an attempt to rake in as much as he can. After all, at that time he would not be receiving a pension when he retired from the game. Things are better nowadays. Wayne had known how to play cricket for a long time, but organising a benefit season was an altogether different ball game. Frankly, he did not do much about it. His committee was a loosely grouped set of friends: David Guest, Ann Long (the landlady of the Coach House Hotel) Steve 'Chalky' White (a close friend) and Brian Barron, a Northampton publisher. The latter organised a brochure with a suitably curly-haired and bristly moustached cartoon of Wayne on the cover. Inside there were articles from all his old pals on the cricketing circuit, such as Geoff Cook, Peter Willey, Graham Gooch, Mushtaq Mohammad, and there was a fine introduction from Peter Clifton of the *Chronicle & Echo* and a marvellous short article by Matthew Engel, formerly a Northampton cricket journalist and latterly the respected editor of *Wisden Cricketers' Almanack*. Matthew observed:

> There was always an easy grace about his cricket and only Gower among his contemporaries has ever matched Larkins in that ... Gooch is the only other Englishman whose murderous mood can compare with Larkins in top form. A bit of Gower, a touch of Gooch - it ought to be a matchless recipe, but still his career has not reached the heights it should have done ... but I would take the memory of his cover drive to my desert island ahead of anyone else's.

More surprising perhaps were contributions by Viv Richards and Geoff Boycott. The former was good enough to send in a hand-written six hundred word article in which he spoke of Wayne and Geoff Cook being the most dangerous opening pair on the county circuit and Viv went on:

> He's a lovely elegant player ... for such a gifted player he has not played often enough for England. Maybe he needs a long run in the team before he'd do well. As it is, Wayne has been a magnificent, match-winning servant to his county. I've never known him curse a fellow player or cheat on the field. He takes his failures and his moments of bad luck with a shrug of the shoulders, which is a fine example to youngsters.

Geoff Boycott, in his article, was even more generous and showed great insight:

> I find it very puzzling that he has won only six England caps, because there are batsmen

with no more ability - perhaps even less -who have played for their country forty or fifty times. Why hasn't he played for England more often? Some say it's because he plays for an 'unfashionable county' or that he is perhaps destined to be one of the game's unlucky people. That may be the case, but I think the fact that he is such a nice, affable lad works against him. You have got to be single-minded, ambitious and dedicated to the exclusion of everything else, and there are days when that's far from easy to do. As a county cricketer he would be one of the first in my team, a super stroke-maker and a marvellous advert for our game.

Before he was able to settle down to his benefit and his cricket which, he hoped, might bring him back into the England reckoning, Wayne had two other problems. At the end of the soccer season, while playing centre forward for top of the table Buckingham Town against Stewarts and Lloyds of Corby, Wayne was brought down outside the box by the opposition skipper, Jimmy Lamond. 'I had just taken the ball round the 'keeper and he just went in with his studs,' Wayne lamented at the time. 'It was pretty vicious.' The fact that Lamond was sent off was no consolation for Wayne. The ligaments in his ankle were badly damaged and his leg needed to go into plaster, which meant that he did not play serious cricket until June. The County Committee was not amused by this incident, although it was conceded that Wayne was still outside his cricket contract when the injury occurred. The trouble was that he had sustained another football injury at the start of the previous season when he had required twelve stitches in his knee after playing for the Queen Eleanor in the town league and this second occasion was, perhaps, one too many. Wayne was typically unrepentant: 'I have no regrets about playing whatsoever. If I thought I would regret it, I would never have played in the first place,' he told the press. 'But you have to run your own life and these things do happen.'

The second problem related to a court case. At the end of August 1985, Wayne had been driving his car in Leeds during the Northants-Yorkshire match in the company of David Bairstow, the Yorkshire captain and wicketkeeper, when they were involved in an accident at which they failed to stop. In the following December he found himself accused at Leeds Magistrates' Court of driving with excess alcohol in the blood, careless driving and failing to stop after an accident. Owing to the fact that Wayne was unwell, the case was postponed until January 1986, but he was then banned from driving for a year and fined £300. Lack of mobility was about the last thing Wayne needed in this, his benefit year.

No car, a dodgy ankle and a benefit to organise as best he could, all these things were hardly a recipe for success on the cricket field. Wayne suffered the worst season of his career, playing in only seventeen Championship matches, passing 50 twice in first-class matches and ending up with 664 runs at an average of only 26. Despite the lack of input from Wayne the County moved up one place to ninth in the Championship and held on to a creditable fifth position in the John Player Sunday League. There was, however, a strange irony to this season. England had shared the one-day internationals with India where Graham Gooch and a recalled Graeme Fowler had opened the innings, but the first two Test matches at Lord's and Headingley had been lost. After the first match David Gower was sacked as skipper and replaced by Mike Gatting and, while Graham Gooch had held on to his place for the second match, Tim Robinson found himself replaced by the late Wilf Slack. Neither did particularly well, so Peter May and his fellow selectors decided on a bold plan. How about Wayne Larkins? He has had a number of injuries, he is banned from driving his car, he has no form at all, let's recall him – this must have been in their minds when Wayne was recalled to open the batting for the third match at Edgbaston beginning on 3 July, although doubtless they found another more

Another bowler is 'Nedded'. (George Herringshaw: www.sporting-heroes.net)

plausible formula. When his name was announced on the Sunday lunchtime news, Wayne had played seven innings and scored 52 runs at an average of seven point something, and in the media there was total amazement. Even Wayne could scarcely believe it.

On the following Monday he had one more innings to play before the Test, which was the County's second innings against Sussex at Hastings. Trailing by 147 runs on the first innings, the County had been set 321 runs to win. Wayne, opening with David Capel, had immediately been struck on the thumb by a rising ball from Sussex paceman Tony Pigott, which sent him back caught in the gully for a second-ball duck. An X-ray revealed that the bone of his right thumb had been chipped and he was forced yet again to withdraw from a Test match through injury. He felt that he was lurching from one crisis to another. Demoralised, he told the press: 'There was nothing I could do about it. The ball lifted sharply and I was unable to get out of the way.' Allan Lamb, who scored a magnificent 157 off 153 balls to win the match for the County by one wicket, sympathised: 'The wicket was a minefield. Ned's ball went straight through the top of the wicket and it was absolutely unplayable.' Wayne was not replaced for the Test by any of those who had opened for England earlier in the season, but by Mark Benson of Kent, straight from the selectors' Pandora's Box. Predictably, although he performed reasonably well against India, Mark did not get another Test. As with Alan Butcher, who had replaced Wayne in 1979, he joined the select group of players for whom, in the selectors' eyes, but nobody else's, one Test match was a proper trial of a player's ability.

In the course of the 1986 season, Graham Gooch had been the one constant in the England opening pair. Having started with Graeme Fowler in the India one-dayers, he went on to have three different partners for the India Test matches: Tim Robinson, Wilf Slack and Mark Benson. For the one-dayers against New Zealand – 1986 was a season with two touring sides, each with three Test matches – he was first joined by Mark Benson, and then by Bill Athey. For the Test matches against New Zealand another name was taken out of the hat, Martyn Moxon of Yorkshire, who managed to get a brace of matches before being replaced by his Yorkshire colleague, Bill Athey, who had been at number three in the first two games. Poor Graham! Six different partners in only one summer! If it were not so debilitating for England's cricket and for the men who strove to represent their country, the policy of the selectors at this time might even be considered amusing.

It had been a dreadful time for Wayne too. Some of his misfortune can be seen perhaps to have been self-inflicted, but cricketers are often thrown in at the deep end when it comes to organising their benefits and, in fact, some are not really capable of creating the structure that is required. Wayne chose as his benefit match the Sunday League match against Kent at Wantage Road on 27 July and, although he contributed only a modest 31 to the side's total, the County romped home by 100 runs. At the end of the season he had received a benefit worth £36,500, which was probably better than it might have been. Had he been willing to take his courage in both hands and been more pro-active he might have raised very much more because there can never be any doubting his popularity with the people of Northamptonshire. But he found it difficult even to ring up potential donors and sponsors and seemed to hope that his Committee would achieve it all for him. Geoff Cook in the previous year had managed to accrue some £48,000 and, later on, another Northants player was so keen to raise every penny that it is said he even made a charge to the daughter of his primary sponsor for his autograph. That was not Wayne's style and he is doubtless the better man for it; but not better off at the bank.

Wayne might have hoped that he would be included in the England party for the 1986/87 winter tour of Australia. After all, the selectors had sought to bring him into the Test side in July, but his hopes were not fulfilled as the selectors recalled Notts opener Chris Broad, who had played against the West Indies and Sri Lanka in 1984. Why not pull another name out of the hat, they must have argued. Bill Athey and Wilf Slack went along as the other openers, but Graham Gooch decided that he would like the winter off.

At the end of the year Wayne signed another contract with Northants. There had been speculation that he fancied a move to the South Coast, and Sussex, who had lost Gehan Mendis to Lancashire and John Barclay to retirement, were keen to sign him. Northants were delighted to know that he had re-signed and Stephen Coverdale, the secretary, told the press: 'Wayne is a big part of our future plans. He is a quality player and may even still have an England Test career ahead of him.' But for Wayne it was another dismal winter of the pub, van-driving and tidying up the loose ends of his benefit.

10
ARE THE GLORY DAYS OVER?

His failure to regain an England spot after the end of his Test match ban had been most discouraging for Wayne. All his friends have noted that, while he puts on a brave face against adversity, he takes personal failure in the cricket world very badly indeed. The bluff exterior conceals great sensitivity, but Wayne felt, quite rightly, that crying over spilt milk served no purpose and that, now at the start of 1987, he was still only thirty-three and Test cricket was still within his range. Nothing, other than his perceived sense of rejection by England's selectors, was particularly wrong with his life. It was not a disastrous situation. It was perhaps true that he had not maximised his benefit, but the generous Northamptonshire folk had put a fair sum into his bank account, and he had a good summer job, even though the winters were likely to be a trial. It was out of the question that he would be dropped from the Northants side and the salary of a senior professional was now sufficient for him and Jane to eke it out over the whole twelve months, even though some van driving for Work Force helped to put a little more icing on the cake and froth on the beer.

In the spring he told the press in Northampton that, while he would have preferred to be out in Australia with the England side rather than watching replays on the television, he felt that his own chances were still very much alive. It would, however, have been a good tour of which to be a part. England, under Mike Gatting's leadership, were enjoying a good series. They had beaten Australia in the First Test by seven wickets at Brisbane, thanks in part to an exhilarating 138 from Ian Botham, and when the teams moved to Perth for the second match of the series, Chris Broad (with 162) and Bill Athey (with 96) had put on 223 for England's first wicket in the first innings, although the game ended up drawn. In the third match at Adelaide, also drawn, Broad had scored another hundred and Athey a further fifty, so the opening partnership situation for England was, unusually perhaps, rather healthy. Melbourne saw an innings victory for England in the fourth match and Chris Broad recorded his third ton of the series. At Sydney, in the final match, Australia had their revenge by 55 runs, largely thanks to a massive 184 not out in their first innings by Dean Jones, a Victorian whom Wayne would come to meet when they both played at Durham. Apart from fifties by Mike Gatting, David Gower and John Emburey, England's batting had once again assumed its usual frail look.

Chris Broad had ended the series with nearly 500 Test runs at an average of nearly 70, so when Wayne announced to the Northampton press at the end of the tour that he was 'bubbling with enthusiasm and gunning for Broad's England place' his eagerness, however good to see, needed to be taken with a pinch of salt, especially as Graham Gooch, who had declined a tour place and stayed in England to be with his family, was never out of the frame. Acupuncture to Wayne's damaged ankle had proved successful and, most sensibly, he had severed his links with Buckingham Town Football Club and played only recreational football with Hardingstone Athletic. Having managed to avoid any footballing injuries Wayne succeeded, however, in getting himself bitten by a dog while he was jogging on a beach in Portugal, where he and Jane had taken a spring break. On resuming training at Wantage Road, he had then managed to damage a sciatic nerve, so his avowed intentions of beginning what he perceived as something of a come back season after the fiasco of 1986 'with all guns blazing', as he told the press, was not going according to plan.

The guns, however, did blaze for Wayne at the start of the season, but only at county level. A run chase against Hampshire resulted in a score of 269 for 5 and a 5 wicket victory for the County with Wayne leading the way with an innings of 120 scored in 149 balls with 2 sixes and 13 fours. Northants chalked up another victory immediately afterwards, this time against Middlesex at Lord's and Wayne scored 66 of the 94 needed to record a 10-wicket win. Pakistan were the summer's visitors and Wayne was asked to captain the County against them at Bletchley, scoring, sadly, a single in one innings and doing less well in the other. At the end of June, however, runs were needed quickly in the first innings against Yorkshire and Wayne obliged with 101 not out from a total of 138 for no wickets declared. This led to another Northants fourth innings run chase with the promising Robert Bailey scoring a massive 152 not out for the county to win by 7 wickets. Wayne notched up a further hundred against Worcestershire later in the season, but his most remarkable innings – one that he described as the 'innings of his life' in a compilation by Jack Bannister of important innings by well-known batsmen – was his 73 against Warwickshire at Edgbaston in August.

It is perhaps significant that Jack chose to include Wayne in his parade of really great names, confirming perhaps what Graham Gooch had said about Wayne, namely that he ranked among the very best of his time. Jack Bannister begins: 'When a man like Larkins has taken on the world's best fast bowlers unflinchingly for two decades, his choice of *Innings of my Life* assumes considerable significance.' To start with, this was a fairly regulation County Championship match. Warwickshire scored an ordinary 235 in their first innings, to which Northants replied and gained a first innings lead of 59, due largely to a fine 85 by Allan Lamb. The home team did rather better in their second knock and, thanks to 99 from Andy Lloyd, who was run out attempting a single to the incredibly athletic West Indian Roger Harper, they were able to declare at 280 for 5 wickets. Norman Gifford, now captaining Warwickshire after many years at Worcester, left Northants with 31 overs to reach the 222 runs needed for victory. A dreadful storm was brewing up when Geoff Cook and Wayne strode into the middle to start the run-chase. Wayne takes up the story: 'When we started our innings, it looked hopeless. Geoff was soon lbw to Merrick. It was almost eerie to play while the thunder and lightning over the city centre, just two miles away, came nearer and nearer. It was dark, but we stayed out there until, finally, it rained. It was heavy and, as we ran off, I saw plenty got onto the pitch before they could cover it – as if we hadn't got enough problems to cope with.' At this point, with Geoff gone on 9 for one wicket, Wayne had scored 22 out of 38 in 6 overs.

When play resumed, it was almost too dark for cricket as the conditions were quite ghostly with thunder and lightning rolling around the ground. Andy Lloyd, the near-centurion, continues the story: 'Ned's innings was one of the most brilliant displays of correct hitting that I have ever seen. I have seen people slog it around, but these were proper shots – cleanly hit hooks, cuts, drives and pulls. It underlined his wonderful hand and eye co-ordination and, although the game was drawn, the innings made such an impact on our players that we talked about it every subsequent season when someone threatened to play a similar innings. No one did, thank goodness!'

The break for rain had taken 5 overs out of the game. Norman Gifford thought that this would secure his side against defeat, so he decided to crowd the batsmen. Paul Smith, whose final analysis was 10-1-103-3, then went for 16 runs in his first over including a six over extra cover into the Members' Bar. When the last 20 overs began, 184 were still needed and, almost single-handedly, Wayne reduced the target to 150 off 17, 137 off 15, 108 off 12 and finally 99 off 11, when Merrick bowled him. He had scored a further 51 runs after the break off 30 balls. The *Birmingham Post* summed up Wayne's innings: 'Larkins cut loose with an innings which, for sheer destructive power and improvised audacity, could not have been bettered – even by an Ian Botham or a Viv Richards.' It made a total nonsense of Wayne's omission from the squad which was to contest the Reliance World Cup in India in the autumn and from the home series of one-day internationals and Test matches in the summer of 1987. Chris Broad and Bill Athey had done themselves no harm by their form in the winter in Australia and they, with some help from Tim Robinson and Martyn Moxon, did most of the opening for England that summer. Even Graham Gooch found it hard to get into the side for more than two matches, but he did manage a place in the MCC side against the Rest of the World in the MCC Bicentenary match at Lord's at the end of August, but had to bat at number three. Nevertheless he did his cause no harm and his 117 almost certainly secured his place for the World Cup squad, where he was restored to the opening slot and, together with either Tim Robinson or Chris Broad, scored heavily and helped take England to the final at Calcutta in November. Sadly, they lost the match to Australia by 7 runs.

Northants enjoyed another profitable season in 1987, attaining a sound seventh place in the Championship and reaching both one-day finals. In the Benson & Hedges Cup they faced Yorkshire at Lord's at the beginning of July and both sides scored 244 runs. Unhappily for Northants, they lost seven wickets in the process, Yorkshire only six. The Natwest Trophy final in September was even more galling. On a Saturday and Sunday, blighted by the English weather, Northants had made a bold start to the match and, with Wayne leading the way with a well-made 87 and, according to *Wisden,* 'batting with style and aggression', they reached 228 for 3 wickets in their allotted 50 overs. In 21 overs on the Saturday evening they reduced Nottinghamshire to 57 for 4 wickets, but they had not reckoned on their opponents' two overseas players, South African Clive Rice and New Zealander Richard Hadlee. On the Sunday morning these two, aided by much good fortune, took the game away from Northants and Nottinghamshire, despite losing seven wickets in the process, reached their target in the final over.

In 1987, John Player and Company had withdrawn their sponsorship from the Sunday League and Refuge Assurance took their place. Northants did not distinguish themselves particularly in the competition and ended up in tenth place. There would be little to comment on in their matches except for one encounter which sowed the seeds of an upheaval in Wayne's personal life. In the winter of 1986/87 there had been stirrings and revolution in the camp at Somerset County Cricket Club. Peter Roebuck, a brilliant student at Cambridge, a highly qualified lawyer and an even keener cricketer, had succeeded Ian Botham as captain of Somerset at the start of the 1986 season. In the course of the season he had become disenchanted with two of his top players: Viv Richards and Joel Garner, the West Indian fast bowler. Taking what was a bold move in view of the abilities of the alleged miscreants, he and the Somerset Committee decided that the two West Indians had become surplus to requirements and should not be re-engaged. In their places Somerset brought in Martin Crowe and Steve Waugh, two players who were, of course, to become icons in the cricket history of their respective countries, New Zealand and Australia. They also dressed more smartly, according to Somerset CCC Public Relations, than the West Indians did. Ian Botham was incensed at the treatment of his good old pal Viv and immediately packed his kit and made off to Worcestershire for the 1987 season.

At the end of the season Worcestershire needed to win their last match to become the first champions of the new Refuge Assurance League, although this new name was about the only thing that was different from the previous season. The mighty Ian Botham had been a plank in his new county's success and had been scoring runs opening the batting with Tim Curtis, later to become his county's captain and the recipient of five England caps, courtesy of the selectors' largesse, in 1988 and 1989, only then to be discarded without further ado. Ian had rented a farmhouse in the back of beyond in Worcestershire, having thrown in his lot with a new county. He decided that, on the evening of the first day of the county match between Worcester and Northants and prior to the Sunday of the vital Refuge Assurance clash, he would hold a large party at his farmhouse to which he would invite both teams and a whole host of his friends from Somerset. Ian Botham's generosity is legendary, but according to Wayne there was also method in his madness. 'Beefy, you know the sort of man he is,' Wayne recounted later. 'Well, he said that he knew how to sort out this Northants side. We'll get them round to my place, we'll have a party, get them pissed up, an all-nighter, and they'll have no chance on the Sunday.' Wayne has always enjoyed a good party and, at this point he was particularly good friends with Duncan Wild, the son of a former Northants player, who had been engaged some years previously and had been capped by the County in the 1986 season. Wayne and Duncan Wild were used to getting up to a few pranks at parties and this occasion was no exception. They were looking for a few more cans of beer and, to reach them, they needed to go through the kitchen to the garage. There they saw Ian Botham's fishing waders and hat hanging up against a wall. Wayne takes up the story: 'I said, Wildy, come 'ere. Do you dare me? I got the hat and the waders, opened the garage door and went out into the field nearby. I got all my gear off and hung my clothes up on a hedge, standing bollock naked in the middle of bloody nowhere, put the waders and the fishing hat on, went back through the garage and into the kitchen, where everybody burst out laughing. I stayed in the waders all night and enjoyed the barbecued steaks, while Beefy poured beer into the tops of the waders, so that I ended up knee-deep in the stuff.'

Wayne was enjoying a bit of attention in his fancy dress and went into one room where there was dancing. Among those present was Debbie Lines, whose husband Richard was a Taunton businessman and one of Ian Botham's associates. Richard had, among other things, helped with the great man's charity walks. Wayne and Debbie started to dance, the former slopping round the floor with all the beer in the waders and their conversation turned to the possibility of going to Worcester races in the following week, but time went on and gradually the party came to an end. Carriages came at dawn and much of what Ian Botham had possibly planned came to fruition. Northants lost out badly in the Sunday League match and Worcestershire took the title. On the Monday and Tuesday Northants lost the Championship match too. Roger Harper and Duncan Wild had scored tons in the Northants first innings, but after pegging Worcestershire back in their first innings, which included a fine 140 not out by Graeme Hick, the visitors collapsed to 101 all out in their second knock and the home side got home by four wickets.

Wayne thought little of his chance encounter until one day in the course of the winter when he went into Wantage Road to do some training and found a postcard awaiting him at the pavilion, which said quite simply 'Worcester Races?' and bore a Taunton postmark. 'I phoned her up and that's how it started. Silly really, I suppose, wasn't it?'

Wayne had missed out on selection for the Reliance World Cup squad nor was he picked for the winter tour of 1987/88 to Pakistan which then went on to Australia and New Zealand. Graham Gooch, Chris Broad, Tim Robinson and Martyn Moxon were England's chosen openers for this lengthy tour, which began in the middle of November in Rawalpindi and did not end until the middle of March in Auckland. England lost the Test series against Pakistan 1-0 with two drawn matches, but triumphed in all three one-day internationals. It was not a happy part of the tour, however, because it contained the infamous exchange of words on the pitch between Mike Gatting, the England captain, and the late Shakoor Rana, the Pakistani umpire. It was an unseemly affair and, now that the dust has settled, it is clear to see that Gatting had a raw deal from the TCCB, who made him write an apology to the umpire even though it was apparent that his part in the row had been much less inflammatory than Shakoor Rana's. Many people now believe that Mike Gatting's removal from the England captaincy after the Trent Bridge Test against the West Indies in June 1988, had less to do with the media set-up which managed to inveigle a barmaid into his hotel room in Nottingham than it did with his row with Shakoor Rana. If this is sadly the case, England lost the best captain they had had since the times of Ray Illingworth and Mike Brearley.

In the second leg of the tour, England drew four Test matches, including the Bicentennial Test against Australia at Sydney, and narrowly lost a series of one-day internationals. At this time the England side was becoming reasonably well set and, while Wayne's omission from their affairs was, from his personal point of view and from his past record in first-class cricket, quite regrettable, it is none the less easy to see how the situation developed.

Recognition for his achievements did not desert Wayne altogether. In December he was a guest of honour in London at a lavish celebration which, among other awards, was recognising his sizzling 101 not out against Yorkshire in the summer. Having enjoyed himself thoroughly and carrying his £1,000 trophy in a bag, on his way home he popped into the Queen Eleanor for his usual swift half to conclude his triumphant day. When closing time came, several swift halves later, he found to his dismay that the dazzling trophy was no longer in his possession. After about fifteen minutes of manic searching and profuse perspiration, Wayne saw his friends producing the trophy from behind the bar!

Before the winter ended there was a further happy event in the Larkins household. Amy Louise was born at the beginning of February at Northampton Maternity Home. Wayne's domestic responsibilities seemed to be increasing at a time when he was feeling an insecurity in his personal life.

Would Wayne make an international come-back in the 1988 season? Or were the glory days over for ever? The latter scenario seemed, sadly, to be the more likely. At least he had the consolation of becoming Northamptonshire's vice-captain now that wicketkeeper George Sharp had retired from the game. At the start of the season the County had signed the thirty-eight-year-old Australian fast bowling legend Dennis Lillee as an overseas player. Lillee thought that he had been engaged to coach, but the County soon made it clear that they expected him to play. Geoff Cook recalls how, when Lillee arrived, he sought to work off some of his jet lag in the nets. He joined Wayne on the artificial wicket at Wantage Road and for well over an hour Lillee bowled his fastest and Wayne batted with all his usual skill.

Wayne, hoping for an international return in 1988. (George Herringshaw: www.sporting-heroes.net)

Hosts of people came round to watch what turned out to be a world class competition. Geoff quoted this event for one reason only; namely, that critics had often suggested that Wayne never bothered to practise. Geoff takes a different view. While acknowledging that Wayne believed that the individual needs to practise in his own way, he also accepted fully that there was a need for team practice and in this he always participated fully. He batted in the nets as seriously an anyone, and Geoff is clear that Wayne would not have maintained his skill, his timing and his technical excellence without a great deal of practice.

The County made a solid, but not spectacular, start to the 1988 season, although Geoff Cook was struck in the face by England pace bowler Graham Dilley and had his jaw broken in the match with Worcestershire in May. This was a repeat of his misfortune when something very similar occurred when he was facing David Thomas at the Oval in 1984. One man's bad luck is another's good fortune and Wayne found himself captaining Northants for the first time for a relatively extended period of matches. Wayne had always believed that he had the tactical acumen and the motivational powers to do the job and many found his leadership excellent, even quite inspiring. While his captaincy in both the Championship and the one-day competitions proved popular, largely because he consulted well, his own form in the first half of the season was very patchy indeed. His one serious contribution was at Taunton where, with the County needing 134 to win, he defended well under a pewter grey evening sky and completed the task in the sunlight on the following morning with a sparkling 81 not out. This secured a seven wicket victory for his side. While in Taunton he had renewed his earlier acquaintance with Debbie Lines – perhaps this improved his form.

Apart from scoring 134 with a six and 24 fours – an amazing 76% in boundaries – against Gloucestershire at Bristol in a one-innings match, which the County narrowly won, and notching up a further ton against Kent at Wantage Road, Wayne did very little in 1988. Geoff Cook, returning to the captaincy after his injury, dropped Wayne for the last two Championship matches of the season. Some time elapsed before anyone got round to telling him why.

Geoff Cook's final year of captaincy was a disappointment for him. In the Championship the County sank from seventh to twelfth place, they were knocked out of the Natwest Trophy in the first round by a minor county, Cheshire, they failed to reach the quarter-finals of the Benson & Hedges Cup and they dropped four places in the Sunday League. The real debate, however, was the question of Geoff's successor. The obvious candidates were Wayne, who had shown a somewhat unexpected flair for the task, Nick Cook, a left-arm spin bowler who had come over from Leicestershire, and Allan Lamb, now well established in the England side.

George Sharp, who had been the County's vice-captain before Wayne, has analysed the

Northamptonshire County Cricket Club, 1988. From left to right, back row: A. Roberts, W. Noon, M.R. Baker, A. Penberthy, D.S. Hoffman, M.A. Robinson, N.A. Stanley, G. Smith. Middle row: R. Norman (physiotherapist), A. Fordham, M.R. Gouldstone, S.J. Brown, D. Ripley, W.W. Davis, D.J. Wild, A. Walker, R.M. Carter (coach). Front row: R.J. Bailey, D.J. Capel, A.J. Lamb, G. Cook (captain), W. Larkins (vice-captain), R.G. Williams, N.G.B. Cook. (Bill Smith)

role of the captain with some acuity. He sees that there are basically two sorts of captains, those like Jim Watts and Geoff Cook, who tread a solitary path and are perhaps rather 'schoolmasterly' in their approach, but who are basically sound tacticians; and others like Mushtaq, Allan Lamb and, of course, Wayne who, while making the odd tactical error, are very much one of the team and inspire great loyalty amongst their fellows. He is certain that Wayne would have been an excellent captain and this is also the view of Geoff Cook. In the end, the Committee's accolade fell upon Allan Lamb and the County prospered under his leadership. Nick Cook probably fell by the wayside because, as a spin bowler in a world dominated by faster men, he was not always sure of his place, but why Wayne was unsuccessful is more enigmatic. Wayne is quite sure that he was offered the post, but declined it because of the turmoil in his domestic life. This is consistent with his own often stated desire to ensure team success over personal advancement, but there may be other reasons too. Knowing of Wayne's domestic situation, did the Committee judge him too preoccupied? Or did they just go for their best player, Allan Lamb, regardless of the fact that England calls might often take him away from the team?

Wayne's domestic arrangements were certainly a mess. Late in the summer Debbie Lines arrived with her two daughters in Northampton and took up residence in the Coach House Hotel. Not long afterwards, Wayne joined them there. This brought a sense of outrage to Jane Larkins and it is clear that she had a point. She may perhaps have enjoyed a life that she might not otherwise have had by being married to a man of some modest, but actual, repute, and they may not always have got on together in public, but she had two daughters at her side, one aged seven and one barely seven months. It was a truly unhappy turn of events.

Wayne's response to his situation, that was at least half self-inflicted, was typical. He may be, in all matters away from cricket, casual, and arguably even feckless at times, but there is a certain understanding in him of what is right and what should be. He immediately made over the whole of the family home in Hardingstone to Jane and his daughters; there was no question of half a house each, as is the case in many marital break-ups. He also handed over to Jane such accumulated funds as they possessed and, almost penniless, took Debbie and her two daughters off to live in Dolphin Cottage, a romantic retreat on the green in the village of Kingsthorp just to the north of Northampton. These somewhat quixotic moves were doubtless right and proper, but his currently insecure financial state stems directly from the break-up of his marriage.

Ann Long, at the Coach House Hotel, who had done so much to help Wayne's benefit season, was an interested spectator at the time. She recalls Wayne's determination to limit the damage of his actions, his rising at 6.00 a.m. to go off and drive a Work Force van throughout the day and his change from liberal drinker to virtual tee-totaller – perhaps almost his sense of penance.

The England selectors had not troubled Wayne since 1986, when he was recalled to face India and had to cry off with a damaged finger. They ignored him in the following season and also in 1988, when the West Indies were again the visitors. England won all three one-day internationals, but the Test matches proved the accustomed disaster and were lost by four matches to nil with one match drawn. Mike Gatting, England's current and often successful captain, fell foul of a press set-up at Nottingham and was replaced by John Emburey for two matches, who in turn gave way to Christopher Cowdrey for the fourth encounter. When the latter was injured and failed to beat the count, Graham Gooch took over at the Oval in August. This heralded the impending, although not the actual, start of

Wayne and David Capel enjoy a drink at the Harrogate Festival. (David Capel)

his long occupancy of the post which was soon to have a beneficial impact on Wayne's career.

For the time being, however, his new personal life probably left Wayne unconcerned about winter tours. There was, in fact, no tour for Wayne that winter or for anyone else as it turned out. A party which was due to tour India was selected with Graham Gooch as captain, but the Indian Government became involved and refused to grant visas to eight of the sixteen players on account of their alleged sporting links with South Africa. The TCCB, holding to the International Cricket Conference's principle that no country should be allowed to influence the team selection of another, refused to replace the players and the tour was cancelled. This was a particular shame for Rob 'Basher' Bailey, Wayne's colleague at Northampton, who, having made his Test début at the Oval, was hoping for his first overseas tour.

Autumn changed to winter. Wayne drove his parcel vans and lived with Debbie in their cottage at Kingsthorp, not far from the Allan Lamb residence. Winter gave way to spring and the start of a new season. The Australians were the summer visitors in 1989. The new chairman of selectors, Ted Dexter, the former Sussex and England captain and motorcycle enthusiast, did not want either Mike Gatting or Graham Gooch as captain and, despite contrary advice at Lord's, appointed David Gower. The series of three one-day internationals were shared owing to an unusual tie in the second match, but once the Test matches started, the Australians started to take hold of things by the scruff of the neck. Despite a fine 125 by Allan Lamb in their first innings of the First Test, England were unable to match Australia's mammoth total and went down easily by 210 runs. England's sorry form continued at Lord's in the Second Test and, although they scrambled a draw in the third match at Edgbaston owing to some typical English summer weather, the fourth and fifth matches went the way of the first two and in the sixth (and final) match at the Oval, the weather again helped England to salvage a draw.

Graham Gooch had opened the England innings in five of the six encounters, twice with Chris Broad, twice with Tim Curtis and once with John Stephenson of Essex, who secured his one and only England cap at the Oval and was to found the 'One Test Wonder Club' in 1996. In the Fifth Test, Graham Gooch had been left out 'to discover his form with his county' and Tim Curtis and Martyn Moxon faced the Australian quicks. A disastrous Test summer ended in the gloom of London SE11. David Gower announced that he would 'ponder his position' as captain: one must assume that he did, but he never captained England again. Ted Dexter, the chairman, told what *Wisden* describes as a 'defeat-sickened nation': 'I am not aware of any mistakes I've made'. Heaven knows what would have happened had he been aware of any.

The County season began with a bang for Wayne. A fast hundred against Oxford University was followed by a number of half-centuries before he reached his first Championship ton at Maidstone. He also scored an excellent 84 when the Australians came up to Wantage Road in a match in which Allan Lamb was injured. Allan had played for England in the one-day internationals and in the First Test, but this recent injury and others subsequently kept him off the park for a fair part of the season. This gave Wayne an opportunity to show his leadership skills as vice-captain and, in fact, he led the County on over twenty occasions in Championship and one-day matches. It was not a bad season

Wayne putting at Cold Ashby Golf Club, to sponsor the British Olympic Appeal.

for the County either. Northants moved up seven places to fifth in the Championship, managed quarter-final places in the Natwest and Benson & Hedges competitions and went up eight places to joint sixth in the Sunday League. Leadership had not affected Wayne's own form and, with a hundred for MCC against Michael Parkinson's XI in the Scarborough Festival at the end of August, he ended the season with 1,787 runs, a total which only the South African, Jimmy Cook, playing for Somerset, exceeded.

At the conclusion of the 1980s, it is interesting to note Wayne's input into English batting. In those ten seasons he scored just two runs short of 15,000 first-class runs, a figure exceeded only by Graham Gooch and Mike Gatting – the latter, in any case, by only a whisker. One might have thought, not even with hindsight, that Wayne's considerable gifts might have been recognised by the England selectors. It is, for instance, instructive to analyse the manner in which they dealt with the question of opening batsmen from the time of their picking Wayne for the Third Test against India in 1986 where, of course, he did not play owing to a thumb injury from the bowling of Tony Pigott of Sussex, until the end of the 1989 season. During that period fifteen players, who were opening batsmen in their county sides, were used by England, often in a wholly random mix. The 1986 season saw Graham Gooch with six different partners in the Tests and one-day internationals and, although the period from the 1986/87 winter through to the following year saw some consistency, when only Chris Broad, Bill Athey and Tim Robinson plus Graham Gooch (when he was prepared to tour) were in the frame, things came to a head in the 1989 season. Nine different opening batsmen, ten if one includes Chris Tavaré who sometimes opened and was recalled for one match, appeared in that season when David Gower was used as an opener in one-day internationals and players such as Kim Barnett of Derbyshire, Tim Curtis of Worcestershire and Martyn Moxon of Yorkshire were moved in and out of sides like pawns on a chessboard. Only Graham Gooch had been any sort of fixture in the side throughout the period in question. By 1989 the selectors were, of course, under pressure, particularly after England's disastrous performances against the West Indies in 1988 and against Australia in the following season. The press and TV pundits, to say nothing of the cricket supporters in the stand, were calling for changes. *Wisden* takes an ironic view, saying that the selectors 'responded to calls for new blood with little more than a smear.' That is quite true; they shuffled largely the same players in and out of sides without any hint of team-building. Of course, it was not only in the opening batsmen area that they tinkered. Bowlers also came and were then discarded, while the five wicketkeepers of the period were shuffled about with no apparent rhyme or reason.

But it had been an excellent season for Wayne Larkins and more good news was to follow. England were due to take part in the Nehru Cup in India in the autumn of 1989 and to tour the West Indies throughout the winter. When the two squads for the tournament and the tour were announced, the name of Wayne Larkins was in both! Reincarnation? Life after death? It was an apparently perverse recall for a man aged nearly thirty-six when younger men were being discarded. Whatever the reason, it was a turn-up for the books for Wayne and very welcome indeed. The glory days were, apparently, not over yet.

11

REINCARNATION

Ten years after his last tour and eight years after his last Test, Wayne found himself, at the age of thirty-five, recalled to the England ranks. Eighty-eight Tests had in the meantime been completed. It was a record of sorts, but not one to be especially happy about. Wayne was obviously elated, as late is always better than never in anyone's books. 'I was hoping to get another chance,' he told the Northampton press, 'but it was beginning to look unlikely. It was certainly a surprise, but having said that, I have performed as well this season as any England qualified batsman. This is the final chance of my career and I am taking it with both hands.' The facts are really rather different. His selection ought to have come as soon as his ban for visiting South Africa had expired, and that is not just hindsight. It is a reflection of the way cricketers have been treated by England's selectors over many years. Sadly, the higgledy-piggledy, try-any-expedient method of pulling Test cricketers out of the mass of some four hundred contracted county players was to go on for quite a few years after this. A cat trying to extract a goldfish from a bowl will often do better. Micky Stewart, the England manager at the time, sums it up neatly in the sad and forlorn way men who have made bad mistakes often do: 'Larkins was a 'nearly' man for three years. No selection meeting ever went by without his name coming up. In the last World Cup he was almost selected and should have been.' No further comment is required.

Why did Wayne make it this time? The reason is quite simple. Someone who had the nous to see talent when it existed and who would put some trust in his views when he reached a position of influence had arrived on the scene. This was, of course, Graham Gooch. Wayne and Graham had been friends since the time they had played in an Essex *v.* Huntingdonshire match at under 16 level, when Graham had kept wicket and batted at number eleven! But this was no case of nepotism. Those present at the selection committee meeting will confirm that the choice of Wayne simply came down to the batsman with whom the skipper would feel happiest opening the innings. That batsman was Wayne. There were some other plus points too: the selectors had picked only two opening batsmen for both parties and that meant that, barring a total collapse of form, Wayne would be assured of a first team place throughout. And for the West Indies leg, he would be in the company of three of his Northants team mates: David Capel, who had begun his Test career against Pakistan in 1987 and had been a member of the touring party to Pakistan and New Zealand two winters previously, Rob Bailey, who had missed his first tour when the India trip was cancelled and, of course, Allan Lamb, who had been promoted to the positon of England's vice-captain.

Before the Nehru tournament began in earnest there were two trial matches for England. The first, at the Karnal Singh Stadium in Delhi, was against Indian Railways who, two years previously, had unexpectedly reached the final of India's Ranji Trophy. Drawn from the 1.7 million employees of Indian Railways, an employer only equalled in its numbers by the Russian Army and the British National Health Service, England were determined not to be shunted off the rails. The ticket office managers, porters and accounts clerks were no match for Wayne, who belted a quick 103 out of a total of 263 for 4 wickets before Graham Gooch had him retired. In the second trial against Air India the same fate befell Wayne. Opening with Graham Gooch he reached a quick 55 before again receiving his marching orders, while the skipper went on to score a well-made 90.

England were, therefore, in fine fettle as they met Sri Lanka in the first match of the tournament proper at Delhi's Colta Stadium. Sri Lanka reached a moderate 193 before being bowled out in the forty-ninth over and England knocked off the runs for five wickets with Robin Smith on an undefeated 81 and Allan Lamb out for 52 leading the way. Wayne, however, nearly ruined his chances by dropping a catch at square leg and chipping a bone on the ring finger of his left hand. It was going to be touch and go whether he would be available for the next match – the real test against Australia at Hyderabad. Wayne, however, was determined to play and this time the heavens smiled on him. He passed a fitness test on the morning of the match.

On the evening before the match a few of the team, Graham Gooch, Robin Smith, Allan Lamb and Wayne, were sampling some lager in the bar and the conversation came round to Terry Alderman, who had bagged Graham's wicket on four occasions out of nine innings in the Ashes series of the previous summer. Many commentators were convinced that Graham was Alderman's rabbit. As Wayne had always felt that he could relate well to Graham he decided to apply his own brand of psychology on the skipper. 'Goochie,' he said, 'this Alderman is crap, he can't bowl, he'll have to disappear. I think he'll be going far tomorrow.' He knew, of course, that Alderman could bowl, but not so well as to dismiss Goochie with such regularity. The drinking continued, but in the morning Wayne woke up to think about his prediction. 'Jesus, I've got to do something about this,' is the way he described it later. 'I've got to back up what I have said.'

Hyderabad's Lal Bahadur Stadium is a lovely ground and everything looked set fair for a good contest, although England were clearly the underdogs, given the thrashing they had received in the Ashes series only a few months back. Allan Border won the toss and decided to bat. Australia's master batsman and tactician had made a bloomer. The wicket played like one at New Road, Worcester at the start of a Championship match in May. The ball swung, moved off the seam and occasionally reared past the batsman's nose, and after 38 overs Australia were struggling at 122 for 3 wickets. At this point Border came to the wicket and joined the off-spinner, Peter Taylor, who had been sent in early to push the score along. In 12 overs the score moved on by 120 runs, with 101 coming off the last ten and 57 off the last five. Border, not really known for vicious hitting, had scored 84 not out off 44 deliveries with 8 fours and 5 sixes. Three of the sixes were off successive balls from Gladstone Small, while Angus Fraser had the indignity of going for a six and 3 fours off consecutive balls. Two of Border's sixes went through the roof of the pavilion enclosure of bamboo wicker-work. As one correspondant noted, a seat out of the sun was no guarantee against a headache! Allan Border was pretty chuffed. 'I felt that I had had a day out,' he said.

England were very much on the back foot when Graham Gooch and Wayne opened the England innings to chase the 243 needed for a win over the Australians. Geoff Lawson and Terry Alderman opened the Australian bowling and they were fiercely 'nedded'. Lawson was hooked for six and went for 29 off his first 5 overs, while Alderman was treated like a club bowler by Wayne, completing only 7 of his allotted 10 overs. With the score on 125 for no wickets, Wayne had 81 to Graham's 36, at 170 he had reached 104 to his partner's

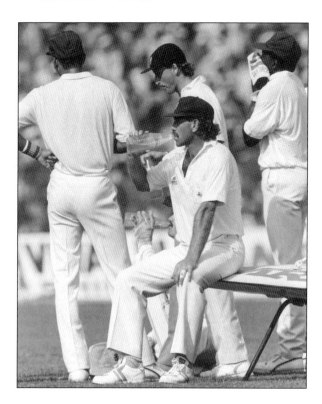

Wayne takes a drink with David Capel, Phil de Freitas and Gladstone Small during England's match with India at Kanpur during the Nehru Cup in 1989. (All Sport)

56, but then at 185 Graham was lbw to Border and six runs later Wayne pushed off-spinner Tim May off his legs and was caught at short mid-wicket for 124. His innings had lasted only 126 balls, had contained 2 sixes and 18 fours so that the enclosure roof now looked more like a bamboo colander. Robin Smith, Allan Lamb and Alec Stewart had no difficulty in taking England to a resounding seven wicket victory. Graham Gooch was lavish is his praise: 'Ned is one of the best batsmen in the country and has been for some years. I doubt if I have seen a better innings in international one-day cricket.' Allan Border was equally sporting: 'Larkins played sensationally well,' he said. Wayne, of course, landed the man of the match award, although Border must have fancied his chances half-way through.

England's progress through the tournament was, however, not all glory. Pakistan were well beaten at Cuttack in a low-scoring game, but at Kanpur, despite good innings by Wayne, Lamb and Stewart, they lost to India by six wickets by allowing fast bowler Chetan Sharma to record an unlikely hundred. They then went down at Gwalior by 26 runs to the West Indies, where Desmond Haynes produced an unbeaten century. For all that, they had achieved a run rate second only to India and qualified with the hosts, Pakistan, and the West Indies for the semi-finals. They were, however, not quite equal to the task and lost to Pakistan by six wickets at Nagpur, while the West Indies defeated India in the other semi-final at Bombay. In the final at Calcutta Imran Khan guided Pakistan to a four wicket win over the West Indies despite another unbeaten hundred by Haynes. England had acquitted themselves well enough and there was much talk in the media about the reincarnated Wayne. He was clearly as pleased as punch when talking of his fine innings: 'It was the best innings of my life because it was for my country and it was against a Test attack.' Playing for the team and not for himself was always his style, of course.

The England players enjoyed a short breather at the end of the autumn before they set off, at the end of January 1989, for the West Indies leg of their winter cricket. There was some time for relaxation at home, but there was also a question of preparing for the tour. Graham Gooch and Micky Stewart, England's manager, were absolutely certain that the team needed intensive physical and technical work before they set off, and the whole party attended the National Sports Centre at Lilleshall in Shropshire for this purpose. This was somewhat foreign to Wayne's nature, as he had always prepared for cricket in his own way and was now considered to be one of the 'old school', but he made it clear at the outset that he could get stuck into the training and adapt. While his propensity for a lager and a fag after matches – and for a very long time after matches – might have given some people the impression of an unfit sportsman, the opposite is in fact the case. Wayne was a naturally fit man and rarely came off this standard. In England, not least around Northampton, there were many people who hoped that Wayne's reincarnation would prove successful. One voice was that of Matthew Engel: 'I can't remember a time when I wanted a cricketer to succeed quite so badly.' Yes, it was all down to Wayne again.

When what was described as this 'most highly trained, disciplined, determined and preached at' squad flew into Barbados to begin the tour at the end of January 1990, the whole place was agog with curiosity. Where were Botham and Gower? Why was Gooch captaining the side? 'You here for another whuppin', man?' Did the tourists not realise that only one team (Pakistan in 1988) had won a Test match on West Indian soil in the past decade? Some of the answers were easy. Botham's bowling had lost some of its bite and David Capel, Wayne's Northampton colleague, was seen as a future star (having made a good impression on the 1987/88 tour), while David Gower had been relieved of the captaincy and been branded a failure after the 1989 summer débacle against Australia. By this time, too, Mike Gatting had been inveigled into a 'rebel' type tour of South Africa and taken some well-known names with him, so Graham Gooch was really the only man left in the captaincy stakes. He was no one's choice, but his determination, his caring attitude and his individual counselling to members of his team proved his critics wrong. He was well supported by Micky Stewart, who described the team as one of fighters who wanted to impose themselves on the opposition. The fact that only Graham Gooch and Allan Lamb had been on a West Indies tour before was seen, in some respects, as a positive advantage. The other fourteen could go to sleep to the sound of breakers, as one correspondent put it, and not with the memory of bouncers! There was, however, one weakness in the side and that was the fact that all the principal batsmen were apparently hard-hitting, attacking players. 'Where is your run accumulator?' was one point asked of Chairman of Selectors, Ted Dexter. The questioner received a long blank stare.

The cricket began in the picturesque setting of Basseterre in St Kitts against the Leeward Islands. Graham Gooch and Wayne started off with an opening partnership of 95 and Wayne went on to reach an excellent hundred in five hours. He was rejecting the theory that he had never rid himself of the idea that attack was the only form of defence. With Alec Stewart in the runs too, with an excellent 125, England were able to declare at 444 for 6 wickets and then go on to dismiss their opponents for 256. After a second England declaration the Red Stripe champions were set 402 to win in a minimum of 64 overs. England were, however, given a fright. When the captains called a halt, with 101 runs needed, 5 wickets standing, and 12 overs left, Graham Gooch was probably the more relieved.

After a narrow loss by one wicket to the Windward Islands at Castries in St Lucia, where the England batting buckled in the first innings – Wayne was top scorer with only 31 – the party moved to Port-of-Spain in Trinidad. No result was achieved in two one-day internationals owing to heavy rain, so the tour moved to Jamaica in readiness for the First Test. Wayne and Graham again opened with style and panache and reached 145 before Wayne was out for 45. His skipper then went on to 239, his first double hundred in England colours in first-class cricket, and England ended with 405 to their credit. With a first innings lead of 94, Wayne went in this time with Alec Stewart and reached 124 in 123 minutes with 2 sixes and 15 fours before he 'retired hurt', rubbing his tummy to indicate some possible ailment. Although this gave his colleagues valuable practice time ahead of the Test, the game petered out in a draw.

The First Test began at Sabina Park, Kingston towards the end of February. The odds were against England, but their four-pronged pace attack of Gladstone Small, Devon Malcolm, Angus Fraser and David Capel had West Indies back in their dressing room for 164. Graham Gooch and Wayne now had to turn events to England's advantage. Although Graham went with the total at 40 and Alec Stewart at 60, Wayne batted adhesively on the next morning and at 11.11 a.m. with the score on 111 for 2 wickets, David Shepherd, watching Sky TV at home, must have had his feet high on the table. A drinks break came, and then Walsh had Wayne taken at first slip, but it was a no ball. Shepherd's legs must have been touching the ceiling! Memories perhaps of Keith Boyce and Wayne on 99 at Chelmsford in 1975! But, unlike 1975, when he did reach his ton, fate was not with him and Wayne did not reach his fifty here. On 46, after three hours of tenacious batting, he was rapped on the pads by a Walsh in-swinger and umpire Steve Bucknor adjudged him lbw. Those studying television replays would have seen the ball missing leg stump, but all was not lost. Allan Lamb, who had been 10 not out overnight and who had battled with Wayne in the morning, went on to 132 and Robin Smith contributed 57, as England closed on 342 for 8 wickets. For a second day running the World Champions had come off second best.

England went to a 200-run lead on the following morning, and by the close the England pace quartet had brought the West Indians to their knees at 229 for 8 wickets. Carlisle Best was the only West Indies batsman to reach fifty in either innings. A win, however, was not quite sealed. Only the weather could deny England and it so nearly did. It rained intermittently on the rest day and heavily overnight, so that the fourth day's play was abandoned. But England's prayers were answered and the sun rising over the Blue Mountains heralded a bright and dry morning for the final day. The last two West Indian wickets went down quickly and England needed a mere 41 runs to win. Wayne lost Graham Gooch, caught brilliantly by Gordon Greenidge at backward short-leg, but in such situations he has rarely hung about and, having driven Ian Bishop back over his head, he pushed a single to mid-off at just after midday and England were home by nine wickets. The tabloids had a field day: the *Daily Mirror* rejoiced in 'Larkins' High Noon Clincher', while the *Jamaican Daily Gleaner* showed a photograph of Wayne scoring the winning run with the caption 'Slaughter at High Noon.' More sober journals found 'England Sublime at Sabina'.

Although England had not been 'Reborn in Paradise', as the *Daily Express* put it, it was by any standard a famous victory against the odds. England had beaten West Indies for the first time in sixteen years. 'It is the sweetest moment of my fifteen years of international cricket,' Graham Gooch declared. 'Many people called us no-hopers, but we've proved

England skipper, Graham Gooch, congratulates Wayne after he hits the winning runs against the West Indies in the First Test at Sabina Park, Kingston, Jamaica, in February 1990. (David Capel)

Wayne and Alec Stewart celebrate after the former hits the winning runs against West Indies in the First Test at Sabina Park, Kingston, Jamaica, in February 1990. (Graham Morris)

them wrong. I feel elated.'

There was now a downturn in the team's fortunes. The third one-day international, played at Sabina Park, was lost and when the team moved on to Georgetown in Guyana, another one-day international was lost. But England were one up in the Test series and at Georgetown they hoped to reinforce their lead. Unfortunately the Guyanan weather did not even allow the Second Test to start, so a substitute one-day international was played and lost. Having flown from Guyana to Trinidad, England enjoyed a conclusive win over a President's XI at Pointe-à-Pierre, despite a hundred from the twenty-year-old Brian Lara, and then went on to Port-of-Spain for the Third Test. After losing the one-day internationals and perhaps surrendering the initiative to the West Indian team, England now needed to give it their best shot.

Queen's Park Oval at Port-of-Spain is another attractive West Indian ground, but the pitch is often well grassed. When Desmond Haynes, deputising as West Indies skipper in place of the indisposed Viv Richards, and Graham Gooch went out to toss, both were hoping to win and insert the opposition. The England skipper's luck held and, after half an hour's play, the West Indies were struggling at 29 for 5 wickets. The England pace quartet, firmly led on this occasion by Derbyshire's Devon Malcolm, had their opponents reeling and the England supporters in the Learie Constantine Stand were causing pandemonium. But they had not reckoned on the pint-sized Trinidadian, Gus Logie. Joined by Carl Hooper, Gus started to repair the damage. At 58, however, the first defining moment of the match and perhaps of the series occurred. Logie, beaten by Malcolm's sheer pace, edged towards Wayne at first slip, but Jack Russell, England's 'keeper, dived in front of him. Jack managed to spill the catch. Logie was on 17 and that would have been 58 for 6. In the end he went on to make 98 and the West Indies' first innings closed on 198 – a significant

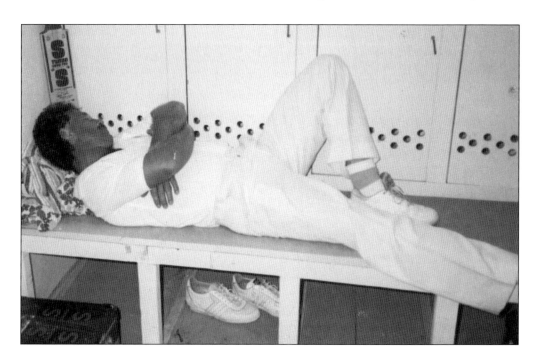

Wayne takes a rest in the dressing room at Port-of-Spain, Trinidad, during the Third Test versus West Indies, March 1990. (David Capel)

achievement by England's bowlers, but it could have all been so much better. Graham Gooch and Wayne batted cautiously until the close when England were 43 without loss, although Desmond Haynes missed Wayne at first slip off Carl Hooper's off-spin in the last over of the day.

The second day of the Test has been called 'one of the least memorable days in the history of cricket at Queen's Park Oval.' Graham and Wayne were keen to show their 'bulldog breed' tenacity and batted through the morning session. After lunch the hundredth run came up in the forty-sixth over before Wayne, having reached his first Test fifty, was caught at the wicket off Ambrose just twenty-five minutes before tea. He had batted for 242 minutes and faced 146 balls. When the occasion demanded, Wayne could be as obdurate a batsman as anyone. Years later George Sharp has commented: 'Larky had a really tight defence, almost certainly better than Lamby's or David Gower's.' At 5.00 p.m., after Alec Stewart had departed in the same way as Wayne, the umpires offered the light to Graham, who had now been joined by Allan Lamb, and off they all went with England on 189 for 2 wickets. Graham had been in all day and scored, unbelievably for him, a mere 65 runs. The press box sought to flay the England team for their tactics, but Wayne was quite vociferous in his defence of what had happened. 'I know there was a load of criticism of what we did today and, of course, they were right to say that we were slow and didn't make all the shots when we could. But I'll tell you what I think. We were determined to wear the West Indies down and we did just that. I want to pay a great tribute to Goochie; he's put a lot of faith in me and, goodness knows, he encouraged me all the time today.' One thing was absolutely sure: England were unlikely to surrender without a whimper as they had done in the previous summer against the Aussies.

Persistent drizzle held up the third day's play for two hours and, when play finally did start, Graham Gooch was out, caught off Ian Bishop for the addition of one run. Bishop had both pace and lift and this not augur well for the rest of England's batting. Allan Lamb reached 30 and David Capel, filling the Botham spot at number seven, hit a well-crafted 40, but England were able finally to secure a lead of only 89 runs. When at the end of the fourth day the West Indies were only 145 runs ahead with nine wickets down, England were still well in with a chance of victory.

If the second day of this match had produced some of the most boring cricket ever seen at Queen's Park Oval, the fifth day exhibited one of the most cynical acts of gamesmanship that has ever despoiled a game of cricket. It was a morning of brilliant sunshine and scarcely a cloud to be seen. Devon Malcolm soon polished off the last West Indian wicket, ending with 6 wickets for 77 runs and ten wickets in the match. England were left with 151 runs to win the match and almost a whole day to achieve it. Wayne went early, caught at the wicket off Ezra Moseley and with the score at 37, Moseley struck again, this time hitting not a wicket but Graham Gooch's hand. It was broken and the second defining moment of the tour had occurred: although he concealed the extent of the injury until well after the match, Graham found himself sidelined for the rest of the tour and Allan Lamb had to take over the captaincy. When the weather, so bright in the morning, turned treacherously to rain at lunchtime, England were 73 for one wicket and still on course for the target. As Alec Stewart, who had come in at the fall of Wayne's wicket and had cut and hooked 6 fours, was walking off the field he was roundly abused by Desmond Haynes, presumably as the result of some niggle on the field. The West Indies looked like going two down in the series and things were becoming nasty. The blue sky over the wooded Mareval Hills, which had promised so much in the early morning,

Wayne batting in the West Indies in March 1990. (Graham Morris)

had soon turned to a dull grey and the slight drizzle became persistent rain lasting for three hours. When it stopped, the ground started to dry amazingly quickly and the umpires decided that play would be possible at 4.00 p.m. with thirty overs bowled.

The West Indians did not want to be playing – for obvious reasons! Surly and unhelpful, they slouched about the field like an Italian football team defending a 1-0 lead, as the *Cricketer* correspondent memorably described their play. At one time seven balls were bowled in twenty minutes, and during the whole two hours' play that actually took place, 17 overs were completed. With the gloom increasing, the third defining moment occurred: Graham Gooch called in his sixth wicket pair, Jack Russell and David Capel and the match was drawn. From then on it was downhill all the way for England.

The scene now moved to the Kensington Oval at Bridgetown, Barbados. A lack-lustre performance against the island side produced a tawdry draw and the fifth one-day international was lost. The Fourth Test saw Carlisle Best score a massive 164 in the West Indies' first innings of 446, Allan Lamb scored his second ton of the series and, in the West Indies' second innings, while Desmond Haynes was grinding out a ton, Lamb tried to slow the match down and resorted to West Indian tactics. It was not a great idea and lost England some of the moral authority, if not actual success, that they had gained in Trinidad. Lamb was supported by manager, Micky Stewart, who told the press: 'You can't retain certain traditions of cricket these days if you are going to be successful. If West Indies bowl eleven overs an hour when they feel like it and then you bowl eighteen an hour, you will come second by a long way.' Thank heavens for the match referee nowadays! Wayne had a disastrous game and avoided a king pair by surviving one ball in the second innings. England, requiring 356 to win in their second innings, failed lamentably and went down by 164 runs.

Inevitably the slide continued. Bowled out at St John's in Antigua in the Fifth Test for a modest 260, they allowed Gordon Greenidge and Desmond Haynes to put on 298 in the West Indies first innings, and in the end they lost by an innings and 32 runs. Wayne scored a sound 30 in the first innings, but went for a mere 10 in the second knock when England had to bat in fading light on the third evening. What had started with such rich promise ended in defeat. The one-day internationals that were completed all ended in England losses and in the Test series they were 2-1 down. Statistics often lie. At worst the England touring party deserved a shared series and, at best, a thoroughly merited defeat of the world champions of Test cricket.

For Wayne Larkins his reincarnation was a marvel. He finished fourth in the Test batting averages and third in the first-class section and had proved to everyone, and perhaps also to himself, that at the age of thirty-six he was a batsman who could mix with the best in the world and have a fair amount to show for it. With thoughts of his wonderful knock in the Nehru Cup and his dogged and determined batting in the Caribbean still in the selectors' minds, he could surely look forward to a full season of Test cricket in the summer of 1990.

Wayne is bowled by Ambrose for 10 in the poor light in the second innings of the Fifth Test at St John's, Antigua in April 1990. (Graham Morris)

12
PARADISE LOST

When Wayne returned from the West Indies to see Debbie and her children at Kingsthorp, he must have felt some real exaltation. At last he could come back home from a Test series and know that he had done well. Awaiting him, however, was a letter, hardly a collector's item as it turned out, which told him that, while he had been away during the winter, his alimony to Jane Larkins and their children had been increased to £600 per month. The reason was that he was now defined as an 'international cricketer'. However much one believed in Wayne and his ability to reach the top of his profession, one had to realise that he was thirty-six and that his time at the top was finite. Although he was to get one further large pay-out as a cricketer in his career, he was going to have to rely on about £30,000 a year as a capped county player and, when that also came to an end, who could tell what would happen?

The 1990 season had two visiting touring teams, New Zealand and India and there would, therefore, be six Test matches and four one-day international matches. Wayne had every reason to expect that he would play in the majority of these matches, if not all of them. He was duly selected for the England thirteen for the first of the one-day internationals against New Zealand at the end of May, despite the fact that his early season form had been abysmal. One run in three knocks in two Championship matches and not too many in one-dayers. Then fate took a hand, almost literally. In the course of a fielding practice at Wantage Road, David Ripley, the Northants 'keeper, had to leave the field and Wayne took over the gloves from him. In a matter of minutes he had stopped a return, which shattered his thumb, and this meant that he did not play cricket again until the beginning of July. His proper international ambitions sank without trace. David Gower was called in to open with Graham Gooch in the one-day internationals against New Zealand, and for the three Test matches an emerging star appeared.

Michael Atherton, from Cambridge University and Lancashire, had enjoyed a successful 'A' Team tour to Kenya and Zimbabwe while Wayne was in the Caribbean, and was called in to win his third Test cap. He had won his first two caps against Australia at the end of the 1989 season, but had missed the boat to the West Indies. He now did everything but miss the boat: 151 in the First Test as Graham Gooch's partner and three more innings over fifty in the New Zealand series. He even managed to play in the two one-day internationals against India later in the season and, of course, he opened in all three Tests against the same opponents, scoring one more ton and two more fifties. To nobody's surprise perhaps, he grabbed his chance with both hands, while Wayne sat nursing one injured thumb. The recently knighted Sir Richard Hadlee was opening the bowling for New Zealand and Kapil Dev for India, but there was always the chance for batsmen to get down the other end and face something of a much friendlier nature. It was not quite like the Caribbean thunderbolts.

Wayne was Northants' official vice-captain, but because of his injury and the fact that Allan Lamb was playing for England, the County was also captained by both Rob Bailey and Nick Cook – unfortunately, it was not proving to be a successful season. When Wayne came back

Wayne in his late thirties.
(David Capel)

Wayne in the course of scoring
58 against Nottinghamshire in a
Sunday League match in July
1990. (George Herringshaw:
www.sporting-heroes.net)

to the County side at the beginning of July, his first match was against Surrey at the Oval. The first day was lost to rain, but on the second day, although more time was lost to rain, Darren Bicknell and Grahame Clinton began a partnership which eventually added 321 for the first wicket. Ian Greig, the Surrey captain, was then able to declare at 347 for 2 wickets and a contrived finish was agreed. Northants forfeited their first innings, Surrey their second and Wayne agreed to chase 348 for a win on the final day. Owing to his only recently mended thumb, Ned had put himself down the order at number five, but he soon found himself at the crease. Three Northants wickets were quickly blown away by Waqar Younis from Pakistan and Martin Bicknell, and Wayne found himself batting with David Capel, his England colleague. David takes up the story: 'We seemed to be batting at the wrong ends. Ned complained that the top order was supposed to be sheltering him from the pace attack and here he was facing Waqar Younis while I was playing the slow left-hand spin of Keith Medlycott.' David did not stay very long, but Wayne went on to reach an excellent 107 with 2 sixes and 18 fours. Last out, when the Northants total was only 200, Wayne came back happily to the dressing room despite the fact that Northants had lost. With his pads still on, he sat down, lit his usual fag, was handed his pint of lager and, looking at his thumb, smiled at David: 'Told you, Capes, it still works.'

Wayne captained the County for much of the rest of the season. Geoff Cook, in his last season before going to Durham as the new Director of Cricket, had agreed to bat lower down the order and Alan Fordham and, occasionally, Nigel Felton, were opening for the County. Northamptonshire's record in the Championship was a disappointing eleventh,

Wayne and Geoff Cook open the innings for the last time together when Northants played Gloucestershire at Northampton in August 1990. Wayne went on to score 109. (Graham Alsop)

Debbie and Wayne enjoy a party at Allan Lamb's house in 1990. Nick Cook, Northants' slow left-arm bowler, is to the left.

they were wooden spoonists in the Sunday League and, although they reached the final of the Natwest Trophy where they lost to Lancashire, it was not a glorious ending for Geoff Cook to savour. The fact was that, with a captain playing Test cricket and a vice-captain out for seven weeks, the team had played under four captains and the cohesion was clearly not there. Counties, however, still seem to appoint their best players as captains even when they know that they will be missing a large proportion of their matches because of England calls.

The season was drawing to a close and wolf-like selectors were prowling around the county grounds in readiness for making their choices for the coming tour to Australia and New Zealand in the winter. Wayne might have felt that his injury and Michael Atherton's obvious success had put him on the back foot and that, once again, he would be denied what he perhaps regarded as his rightful place in the England line-up. But his form in August was good: he hammered a fast 104 against Lancashire on a Sunday at Wantage Road and, when he and Geoff Cook opened for the last time together in the Refuge League match against Gloucestershire at the end of the season, he scored a lightning 109 in 77 balls with 7 sixes and 7 fours, captaining the County to one of its few victories that season.

Of arguably even greater significance was the Championship match against Essex at Northampton right at the end of August. Graham Gooch had scored an imperious 174 in the visitors' first innings and when the home side came to bat they soon found themselves with three down and under a hundred on the board. Wayne, unusually, was batting at number four and proceeded to occupy the crease for five and a half hours, hitting 2 sixes and 27 fours. Although dropped four times, he reached 207, the third double hundred of his career. Doing so in front of the England captain was certainly not a bad idea, but when Wayne's name appeared in the winter touring party for Australia and New Zealand, there were vehement denials all round that the 207 had anything to do with his selection! Northants, with Rob Bailey and Allan Lamb also reaching hundreds, went on to score 592 for 6 wickets declared, which broke the County's record innings total of 557 for 6 wickets achieved in 1914. The declaration on the flat Wantage Road track did not bring any result except that Graham Gooch reached another hundred and completed 2,500 runs for the season and the specatators were bored to tears. Andy Roberts, writing in the *Chronicle & Echo* thought that Lamby might have done better to go on to beat the 631 for 4 wickets, the highest innings total ever recorded at Northampton. Fate plays some strange tricks. When the County went on to Chelmsford nine days later to play Essex again, they beat their newly acquired record with a second innings total of 636 for 6 wickets declared. On this occasion Wayne scored 207 runs fewer!

What seemed at one stage like paradise lost was happily regained by Wayne's chance to go to Australia in the winter and to continue the good work that he had started earlier in the year in the Caribbean. It may not have been those 207 runs at Wantage Road, but Graham Gooch still had faith in Wayne and he needed to keep repaying it.

13

THE COOK REPORT

Geoff Cook was born in Middlesbrough in 1951 and came to Northamptonshire County Cricket Club in 1970, where Wayne Larkins – and Geoff is one of the few people always to refer to him as Wayne – was already on the staff. He made rather faster progress than Wayne and became a first team member somewhat earlier, but they really came together in 1978 when they became regular opening partners. They continued in that role until 1989, becoming the most accomplished and successful opening pair throughout the decade. At that point Geoff, having relinquished the captaincy of the County Club in 1988, a post which he had held for a record eight seasons, moved to the new county of Durham to become their first director of cricket. He played in seven Test matches and six one-day internationals for England in the early 1980s and was seen at that time as a potential England captain. He is better placed than virtually anyone to speak of Wayne Larkins, the professional cricketer, and has produced this short critique:

Wayne's batting statistics do not make fantastic reading, but he did score nearly sixty first-class tons, which is good by the standards of most people. When he got the bit between his teeth he certainly made the most of it and I think that his ability to play match-winning innings is the most important thing about his batting. There are in cricket really two types of successful batsmen: those who score volumes of runs and those who may not score so heavily, but at the end of the season they may well have won three or four matches for you. It is testimony not only to their ability, but also to their desire to undertake something both for themselves and for the team, to accept responsibility for winning the game themselves. I was lucky enough to play with some genuine match-winning batsmen like Allan Lamb and, to a lesser extent at the start of his career, Peter Willey. If you look at Wayne's record you will see this ability shining through as a feature of his game. I think he would be the first to admit that he probably did not score the volume of runs his ability allowed, but that was because he put the emphasis on attack and tried to let Northants or Durham take a dominant position in the game straightaway. It's to the detriment of a team, obviously, if they lose an early wicket or two because of over-zealous play, but more often than not Wayne's assertive attitude at the start of the game put the opposition on the defensive.

It is indisputable that Wayne loved the team environment, loved the team to win, loved the ambience of the dressing room, was very keen to promote team spirit and, in the main, reacted positively to the captaincy of other people. One thing that captains under whom Wayne played might have preferred would have been a greater input into team tactics, constructive comments around the dressing room at relevant times rather than, as happened more often than not, comments after the game or when socialising later at the bar. Perhaps it was his character that made him reluctant to put his head on the block and make constructive comments on team strategy and composition.

I opened the Northants innings on very many occasions with Wayne and I can speak

Geoff Cook, Wayne's captain and opening partner at Northampton. (Bill Smith)

comfortably on partnerships, both from a personal and a general perspective. Everyone found him an easy and enjoyable person to bat with because of his relaxed attitude at the crease and because he was almost invariably able to score runs off most sorts of bowling and take the pressure away from his partner. The three ingredients of his batting were a brilliant batting ability, a good technique and much natural power. When he felt confident – and thankfully, that was most of the time – he exerted considerable pressure on the opposition's bowlers because of his aggressive nature. When you were at the crease with him the team was always on the offensive, and this clearly makes batting very much less pressurised and, frankly, very much easier. He was a great one to offer verbal support, words of encouragement and praise, in fact, all the things you look for in a batting partner. The fact that he himself never looked anxious had a most relaxing effect on those with him. I always found him a good man and a fine companion to bat with, and in many ways we complemented each other in our differing methods of playing. The fact that we were friends as well helped greatly. We had little problem with running between the wickets and he coped with my idiosyncrasies better than most, probably because he was more familiar with them than anyone batting down the order. He was an excellent runner between the wickets and a superb judge of a run. Considering the number of times we batted together, the running calamities were few and I felt buoyed up by the positive influence Wayne exerted. One of the remarkable things about Wayne and myself was that we very rarely talked about our own or each other's batting. The partnership seemed just to have flowered and blossomed naturally – without any effort at all.

The two episodes when English teams went to South Africa in the 1980s were sad ones for English cricket, the first depriving the country of players who were then playing in Tests and of others who would be likely to play in the immediate future. The second had a poor effect, but perhaps for different reasons, as it was all brewing up during the then current season and had an erosive effect on the morale and attitudes of those who were playing for England at the time. The first tour in 1981/2 marked perhaps a watershed in my relations with Wayne and, of course, with Peter Willey. I was captain of Northamptonshire at the time and had agreed, in principle at least, to go on the tour, but after I had spoken to quite a few people inside and outside the game, I was convinced by them that taking part would not be in the best interests of the English game, so, very much at the eleventh hour, I withdrew. Wayne and Peter did not quite accept that my withdrawal was not a selfish move and, consequently, a lack of trust developed between us that has taken a long time to disappear, if ever it has.

I am not quite sure why Wayne did not get back into the England team after his three-year ban. Suffice to say that England used a whole host of players in the 1980s and Wayne was probably as likely to score runs for England as many of those used. When one is assessing cricketers in the Test arena one needs to understand that natural talent means less and less the higher one goes. It is much more how you cope with the whole environment and whether you are judged to be the right person for the particular job. It is impossible to quantify the exact percentages, but if you calculate that first-class cricket demands 90 per cent ability and 10 per cent mental toughness, then the figures for Test cricket are likely to be 60 per cent ability and 40 per cent in the mind. One has to be a strong enough character to cope with the situation, the opposition and the whole extent of the game, and with the exposure to and pressure from the media. It becomes, therefore, the judgment of the selectors whether a particular person can handle all this and is the right man to win international matches for his country. Talent is not everything. The cricketing world is littered with batsmen and bowlers who, on pure talent alone, do not appear to have been given the opportunities that their talent has suggested they deserved.

A person's character is often reflected in the way in which he plays the game. Some people have commented that Wayne showed a certain nervousness in his game despite what was often quite flamboyant batting. It is quite true that he did lack a little confidence early on in his career and was always a notoriously poor starter in a new environment. This may have betrayed him at certain times, but he also showed great concentration when he got the bit between his teeth. After all, he scored nearly sixty first-class hundreds and three double tons. He had a clear view of the way in which he wanted to play, namely, that the ball was there to be hit and the bowling dominated. He was very rarely at the crease for any length of time without his having imposed his personality and his philosophy on the game, yet some critics take a different view. They assert that he gave his wicket away too often by attempting to impose himself, and that a little more circumspection, ambition and steel might have been more appropriate. Yet, if this view had prevailed with Wayne, we would probably have lost many of the incredible match-winning innings that he played.

Getting the balance between assertiveness and caution is never easy, but Wayne was clear that he needed to play the sort of game that he thought was right. He firmly believed that cricket was a game of skill and this was always likely to prevail over the artisan approach. Even when he dabbled with bowling – and he really could have been a much more successful bowler than he was – he always made great efforts to swing the ball and, when it came to fielding, he was always outstanding, catching and running out batsmen in brilliant fashion. He admired the skilful purveyors of the art, men like Gordon Greenidge for instance, and sought to emulate them. In terms of his international career it might perhaps be said that giving the right impression did not always concern him, and he might have applied himself better in certain situations. Getting this aspect of life right might have brought him more Test caps but, being the person he was, with a slightly stubborn streak, he never made any radical alterations to his game or to his attitude. He felt that his skill would prevail over that of other people and, if it did not, he would die by the sword. This made him the cricketer he was, and there can be no doubt that his batting was enjoyed by many people, fellow cricketers and spectators alike, but this aspect of him is almost certainly a factor in why his Test appearances did not match the level of his ability.

Wayne has always been a naturally fit person. You could perhaps compare him in some ways with the Australian batsman Doug Walters, an immensely talented player, but a man who enjoyed some fairly simple pleasures, a pint or two here and a fag there, together with the chance to meet and chat to people at various times of the day. Wayne lived his life as he wanted to. Some of what I have said may well refer to a time a few years back. It was accepted then that cricketers could have a fairly severe night out and still do the job very well. The culture has changed nowadays. Games are much more intense and orientated towards winning. Cricketers have to play to their maximum much more often than was the case in the 1970s and 1980s. In that respect Wayne followed a not irregular trend. People at that time mixed a fairly hectic social lfe with making a living out of playing cricket and it is clear that such a life did play a dominant role with Wayne.

It is certainly a myth that Wayne was not keen on practice, although it is well recognised that he tended to practise in his own way. He was a great believer in the view that the individual needs to prepare for cricket as he wishes. He accepted fully that there was a need for team practice and he always participated, but he thought that each person should also follow his own individual pattern of practice. Some cricketers enjoy the group warm-up, run around the pitch or study the wicket intensely, but Wayne, when he was in form – and that was most of the time – was quite happy to have a few hits on the bat and to continue to chat to people in the pavilion and on the ground. He might have done even better had he followed more traditional schemes of practice; equally he might not have done. But when team net practices were taking place, if a county match was not in progress, Wayne batted as well as anyone and took the whole thing very seriously. He also supported and advised young players enormously well.

When I gave up the Northamptonshire captaincy I was intrigued to see whom the Committee would appoint to succeed me. There were probably three candidates: Wayne, Nick Cook and Allan Lamb. Wayne certainly had the ability, for he had an excellent cricket brain in terms of tactics and match assessment and, in some ways, should have been favourite. The County would have doubtless done well under his leadership. In the end Allan Lamb was chosen and, of course, they went on to do quite well with him.

14

BACK TO OZ

After the vicissitudes of the 1990 season and his generally poor form, Wayne might have expected not to be selected for the Australian winter tour of 1990/91. He had, of course, acquitted himself well in the West Indies in the previous winter and nobody had yet forgotten his 124 in the Nehru Cup in the autumn of 1989. The tabloid press used terms like 'excess baggage' when news of his selection became public, but Wayne was adamant that he had a role to play. 'I didn't get enough credit for my efforts in the West Indies,' he told the *News of the World,* 'I was slagged off when we lost the last two Tests and now I can see why people are trying to call me a waste of space. I am in the side as an experienced opener and aim to do my bit.' There was, however, one significant difference on this occasion. Whereas he had been one of two openers on the West Indies trip, he was now one of three, as Michael Atherton's form against New Zealand and India in the summer had made him a certainty for a tour place. The selectors, too, needed to look to the future, and Atherton, now only twenty-two, had been hailed as an England prospect for some time. 'FEC' or, allegedly, Future England Captain had been hung on his locker in the Old Trafford dressing room, although those in the know thought it meant something quite different and less attractive. There were other candidates, too, for the third opening spot. Darren Bicknell had averaged nearly 75 for Surrey in 1990, while Hugh Morris of Glamorgan had skippered the 'A' team to Pakistan and Sri Lanka in the previous winter and had also enjoyed a successful season for his county. The most likely reason for Wayne's inclusion was further support from the captain, Graham Gooch, who, while thinking that Atherton might open in the Tests, believed Wayne could do another excellent job in the one-day matches of which the tour boasted a multitude.

If Wayne was not officially designated a senior professional on the tour, he was certainly one of the older players. Only Graham Gooch and Eddie Hemmings were his seniors. There must have been some expectation that he would be something of a mentor to the younger players but, although he was always highly popular with them, they may have seen him more as a wag than as a role model. This might have caused Graham Gooch – and Wayne could not have had a better supporter throughout his career – to say at the end of the tour: 'Wayne did not come up with the goods in Australia and that was a pity. With more application and dedication he could have been an outstanding player. He felt that at his age it was better for him to hit a few balls, get the feel of things and then ease himself into his batting out in the middle without too much exertion in the nets beforehand. He felt that experienced players knew how to pace themselves, but I had to disagree. You can't afford to let things drift, to delude yourself into thinking it'll be all right on the night. In the end it was sad for him not to come up to the highest standards.'

Wayne's first room-mate when the team arrived in Perth at the start of the tour was the twenty-four-year-old Philip Tufnell, a left-arm spinner from Middlesex on his England first tour. No sooner had they set their bags down in their bedroom than Wayne went downstairs, only to appear a few minutes later with two cases of Swan lager. 'Fancy a beer?' he asked Phil, but without waiting for an answer he handed him a can, popped open his own can and drank it down without a pause for breath. According to Phil they apparently drank for about an hour as the room gradually filled with smoke and the pile of cans increased. Phil eventually decided to go for a swim in the hotel pool, have lunch and, frankly, check out some of the local talent. Wayne professed his satisfaction with relaxing on the bed, watching the TV and settling down to the cases of lager. 'I'll be right as rain here,' he said to the departing Phil. Later that evening, when the latter returned, the scene was much the same except that the pile of empty lager cans had grown immeasurably. 'Fancy a beer?' Wayne again inquired in his inimitable style. But, as he has always said: 'Prepare for matches in your own way and let the bat do the talking.'

The tour opened in Western Australia with a few warm-up matches of one or two days' duration before the first big occasion against a strong Western Australia State XI. Wayne did not find himself included, which perhaps indicated that he was not, at this stage, in the 'first eleven', but after hammering 110 against a South Australian Country XI at Port Pirie he was selected to play against South Australia at Adelaide. England were soon down to two openers, Wayne and Michael Atherton, as Graham Gooch, who had split his right index finger in taking a return in the Perth nets, found that it had become seriously infected and required an urgent operation. The England XI did little to distinguish themselves and lost by six wickets before moving on to Tasmania to play an Australian XI.

The England team which went to Australia and New Zealand in 1990/91. From left to right, back row: Geoffrey Saulez (scorer), Robin Smith, Michael Atherton, Phil Tufnell, Gladstone Small, Martin Bicknell, Chris Lewis, Angus Fraser, Devon Malcolm, Alec Stewart, John Morris, Lawrie Brown (physiotherapist). Front row: Peter Lush (manager), Jack Russell, Eddie Hemmings, Allan Lamb, Graham Gooch (captain), David Gower, Wayne Larkins, Micky Stewart (assistant manager). (Graham Morris)

Wayne batting for England at the start of the 1990/91 tour of Australia. (All Sport)

Although Devon Malcolm bowled well at the chilly Bellerive Oval in Hobart, the batting, apart from two dazzling tons by acting captain Allan Lamb, was weak and an originally promising position was let slip, allowing the Australians to secure a draw.

England arrived, therefore, for the First Test at the Gabba in Brisbane without a captain and without a win in a first-class match. Allan Border won the toss and had no hesitation in inserting England's rather frail batting. He was proved right. There were, of course, only two openers available, Wayne and Michael Atherton, and neither was in prime form. While Atherton's technique, which had been smooth and assured in the English summer, was being tested by Australia's bouncier wickets, Wayne was not feeling well but he was clear that he had a debt to repay. 'Now more than ever,' he told the press, 'I owe it to the captain to come up with a performance that warrants the faith he's kept in me.' He was, in fact, now suffering from an abscess in his mouth and had endured some well-intended but less than professional treatment for it from Lawrie Brown, the team's Scottish physiotherapist. Sadly, his health and his consequent form were poor and he lost out to Merv Hughes in the first innings and to Bruce Reid in the second. Only David Gower with 61 batted well in England's first knock of 194 and, although Angus Fraser, Gladstone Small and Chris Lewis, with three wickets apiece, had dismissed Australia for 152, another batting collapse ensued and England, all out for 114 in their second innings, left the Australians only 157 to win. Mark Taylor and Geoff Marsh knocked off the runs smartly and without loss.

The England management had flown Hugh Morris over from England to cover the opening spot while Graham Gooch was indisposed, but he was used only in the 'make-weight' games between the important fixtures. *Wisden* heavily criticised the management for not using him more often, but the decision to play, wherever possible, the players originally selected for a squad has always to be seen as sound. Intertwined with the main

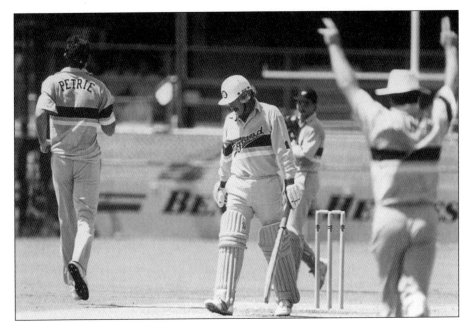

Wayne caught by Young off Petrie for 15 in a World Series match versus New Zealand at Brisbane in December 1990. (All Sport)

Wayne batting for England versus Australia on Boxing Day 1990, while making 64, his highest Test score. (All Sport)

tour – only planners from far away can make such crass blunders – England were involved in a triangular one-day series with Australia and New Zealand. This led to a host of matches against Academy and Prime Minister's XI's mixing in with the one-day internationals all in the middle of the Test series and with relatively few first-class matches, surely the basis for proper practice for Tests, in the programme.

Wayne did not figure in the first one-day match of the series, which England lost to New Zealand, but in the next two he top-scored with 44 in a win against New Zealand and batted well in a match that was lost to Australia. He kept his place in further matches before the Second Test began on Boxing Day but, just like the England team, he did not distinguish himself particularly. Before the next Test began there was one further first-class match – against Victoria at Ballarat. It gave the England team a slight chance to regroup for Test match cricket in the midst of the eccentric fixture list. The hosts piled on the runs in their first innings and, although Allan Lamb made a brilliant 143 in England's first knock, they ended up 78 runs adrift at the half-way stage and, after a second Victorian declaration, they were set 304 runs in 71 overs to win. Despite fifties from David Gower and Robin Smith they finished on a paltry 204 for 7 wickets. Wayne had not been included in this match and it seemed as though he was not seen as a fixture in the Test side, but, as luck would have it, Allan Lamb decided to show how committed he was to the Stewart/Gooch regime of fitness and, while jogging back to the hotel after his innings of 143, he tore a calf muscle, which sidelined him for two Tests.

The second Test began, therefore, in the warmth of Melbourne on Boxing Day in front of 50,000 spectators and with Wayne filling the number three slot. Michael Atherton quickly went for a duck and Graham Gooch, albeit briefly, re-emerged as Alderman's rabbit. He padded up and was adjudged lbw for 20. Wayne added 79 with Robin Smith and a further 43 with David Gower before he was fourth out at 152 for a well-made 64, his best score in Tests. For a batsman whom the management obviously considered as suitable only for one-day matches, he batted with great patience for three and three-quarter hours. His colleagues have always considered his defence to be tighter than that of many other Test players and the lessons he had learned in blunting the West Indies quicks in Jamaica and Trinidad were clearly in evidence. A David Gower hundred and an impetuous 79 from Alec Stewart finally took England to a respectable 352. With Angus Fraser taking six Australian wickets for 82 runs, England enjoyed a possibly unexpected first innings lead of 46. But all was not well. In the second innings Michael Atherton again went cheaply and, although Graham Gooch and Wayne added 86 for the second wicket, the innings disintegrated thereafter. Wayne, batting 232 minutes for another patient fifty, welded the middle part of the innings together for a short while, but, when he was sixth out for 54 with the score on 148, the rest of the innings faded away. Incredibly for a Test side, four further wickets fell for just two more runs. Graham, with 58, and Wayne had made 112 of the 134 runs made off the bat by England. Needless to say, the Australians knocked off the 197 runs required to win for two wickets and in no time at all.

In the modern parlance the Second and Third Tests were 'back-to-back' and the two teams met again at Sydney four days after the conclusion of the last match. The fixture list allowed a quick day-nighter on New Year's Day in which England again lost to Australia, although Wayne again top-scored with 40. He retained his Test place because he had batted so adhesively in the Second Test and Allan Lamb remained on the sidelines. Allan Border won the toss and batted. Although the England bowlers made steady inroads into the Australian batting, they were unable to stop off-spinner Greg Matthews, in at number seven, scoring a

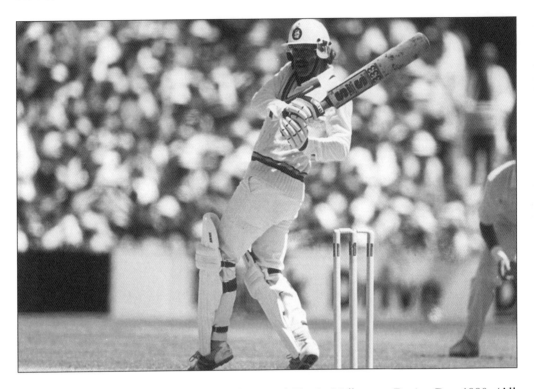

Wayne hooks during his innings of 64 in the Second Test in Melbourne, Boxing Day 1990. (All Sport)

good 128 and the innings closed on 518. England started well: Graham Gooch and Michael Atherton made 95 for the first wicket, but not long afterwards Wayne's tour came to a virtual end. Atherton pushed a ball straight to Allan Border at short mid-wicket and called Wayne for a run. He responded, but was easily run out as Border scored a direct hit on the stumps at the 'keeper's end. He had gone for 11. Much could be inferred from this incident. Was a young opener seeing off an old warhorse opener or was it just a bad call? Wayne, to his credit, is adamant that it was an error, but it was, by any cricketing standards, the most inept of calls and it effectively closed Wayne's Test career. Atherton went on to make a dogged 105 in 451 minutes – the slowest ton in Ashes Tests – and, with David Gower contributing another cultured hundred and Alec Stewart a well-made 91, Gooch was able to declare 49 runs behind on 469 for 8 wickets. The Australians, for a moment at least, seemed to lose the psychological advantage, lost two wickets overnight and were dismissed in their second knock for 205 with Phil Tufnell recording an excellent 5 wickets for 61 runs. This left England needing to score 255 runs for victory in twenty-eight overs, an impossible rate of 9.1 runs per over. Gooch and Gower added a brisk 84, but when Wayne came in at number three he took up the challenge immediately and, in attempting to sweep Allan Border, was adjudged lbw for a duck. So, eleven-and-a-half years later, he walked back to the pavilion just as sadly as he had done when given out lbw to Joel Garner in the final of the World Cup in 1979 and out of Test cricket forever.

Wayne played another day-nighter against Australia on 10 January and a first-class match against New South Wales at Albury, which ended on 16 January. After that he was ignored until the end of the tour in Auckland, New Zealand in the middle of February. 'The amazing thing was,' he mused much later, 'that nobody ever said a single word. No reason why I was dropped from the Test team, no reason why I did not get a single one-day match in New Zealand, nothing. I was just left to draw my own conclusions. I always played for England with great pride and it was an unhappy end.' It was, of course, true that Allan Lamb was by then fit and had come back into the side, but Wayne had scored 141 runs in three Tests, Robin Smith only 74. It was perhaps a case of giving the younger man a chance, but the lack of communication was inexcusable. There is perhaps an irony in the fact that, later into the 1990s, Robin Smith himself was unceremoniously and wrongly dropped from England's Test team at a time when his powers were undimmed and his batting average higher by far than that of any other England player.

There was perhaps some consolation for the England players on the social front. The wives and girlfriends had been allowed to join the team over the Christmas period and Debbie and her daughters were pleased to see Wayne again. Despite the wretched news of injuries and poor form on the cricketing front, the festive season was not allowed to pass uncelebrated. There was the usual fancy-dress party with, among other colourful disguises, Allan Lamb, dressed in fishnet stockings as a Bunny Girl, David Gower as Biggles and John Morris as Archbishop Tutu. Debbie and Wayne, dressed respectively as Napoleon and Admiral Horatio Nelson, enjoyed the social whirl.

Wayne, Debbie and her two daughters, Elly and Carly, enjoy the social side of an Australian tour.

The Prime Minister
The Honourable R. J. L. Hawke, AC MP
requests the pleasure of the company of

Mr Wayne Larkins

at a Reception
on the occasion of
the Prime Minister's XI *v England*

at The Lodge
on Monday, 3 December 1990
at 6.00 p.m.

R. S. V. P.
The Ceremonial Officer
Department of the Prime Minister and Cabinet
Canberra A.C.T. 2600
Telephone: 06 271 5341

Invitation for Wayne to a reception in Canberra on the occasion of the Prime Minister's XI versus England, during the 1990 Australian tour.

For all the frivolity on the social scene, the tour did not end happily. England drew the Fourth Test, thanks largely to some excellent batting by Graham Gooch, who made 117 in England's second innings, but the final Test was a disaster with Australia romping home by nine wickets. When the party moved on to New Zealand for the final leg of one-day internationals the news was hardly better. The hosts won the series by two matches to one, and a tired and, in many respects, dispirited England party flew home. Former Australian Test stars aired their views to the media. Doug Walters, who played 74 times for Australia, called it the worst performing England side he had ever seen. 'It's about time they went back to what they were taught and played down the line of the ball,' he told the press. Keith Stackpole, a former opening batsman and vice-captain of Australia in the late 1960s and early 1970s, chimed in with 'In my day I used to be amazed how people like Cowdrey, Barrington and Dexter caressed the ball. The current crop just lack technique and try only to smash the ball to the boundary.'

When the party arrived back at Heathrow, the traditional airport press conference failed to materialise. Hurrying to a waiting car with his wife and family, Graham Gooch said: 'There's not too much more to say.' He was undoubtedly right.

15

FLYING THE NEST

Wayne was now divorced from Jane, and Debbie from Richard Lines. They were happy in their cottage on the green at Kingsthorp with Debbie's two daughters, Elly and Carly, but there was the question of Wayne's professional career to consider. He recognised rather sadly that his Test career was now over. He had felt bitter about the manner in which it closed, but very sensibly took the view that tomorrow is another day. But there was an even more pressing question. How much longer could he continue with Northamptonshire County Cricket Club? Would they not soon wish to introduce younger players onto their staff? Was a batsman who was going to turn thirty-eight in the autumn likely to be a part of their long-term plans, however good his county form and however keen he was to remain a professional county cricketer?

Wayne had been informed at the end of the 1990 season that he had been relieved of the vice-captaincy and that Robert Bailey would succeed him. Stephen Coverdale, the Northants secretary, explained that it was considered a progressive move and that it was right for the County to look forward. He implied that Wayne had felt a sense of relief at the change and added diplomatically: 'I would not say that the Club has been disappointed with his vice-captaincy.' It was announced simultaneously that Mike Proctor, the South African all-rounder and one of a number of great cricketers to miss out on Test careers because of *apartheid,* had been appointed director of cricket. New brooms tend to sweep clean. Wayne still had two years of his contract to run, but he spoke to Coverdale to inquire whether he might approach Durham to see if they would be interested in obtaining his services. After all, Geoff Cook, his old opening partner, was now there in an executive position and it was clear that Durham would need to take on some more experienced players to reinforce their home-grown talent if they were going to make any impact on the first-class scene. An agreement with Durham was soon reached.

Before all that, however, the 1991 season had to be faced. It was unlikely to prove to be a great season for Wayne. The County was interested in looking at a new opening pair. Alan Fordham, a product of Bedford Modern School and Durham University, had come onto the staff in 1986 and been capped in 1990. He had scored over 1,600 runs, including a double ton, in the previous season and had, to all intents and purposes, taken over the Geoff Cook role. Nigel Felton had started his career with Somerset, moved to Northants in 1989 and had done well enough to be capped in 1990 as the result of scoring nearly 1,500 runs. Wayne, therefore, was not necessarily number one opening bat any longer. In fact, in his first Championship match against Essex in May, he found himself batting at number six. For the next game, however, against Leicestershire at Wantage Road, he found himself back at the top of the order and, when he had scored 21, he became only the fourth Northamptonshire batsman to score 20,000 first-class runs for the County. Wayne had joined a select band of Jack Timms of the 1930s, Dennis Brookes, just post-war, and, of course, Geoff Cook. But his pleasure was short-lived. When he had reached 39 a lifting ball from David Millns, the visitors' opening bowler, broke his right thumb. It was the same old story of injury, and a further period of inaction confronted him. He did not play again until the end of July, and from then until the end of the season it was a fairly desultory performance. In August a good undefeated 62 in winning the match against Yorkshire by nine wickets and a crisp 75 with 1 six and 13 fours against Warwickshire in September were the highlights. Strangely, he found himself not out in more innings than is customary for an opener and of his sixteen knocks six were undefeated so that his modest 365 runs translated into a respectable average at the end of the season. His form on Sunday afternoons was a good deal better. A sparkling 108 in 94 minutes with 11 fours and 1 six against Essex in August was accompanied by three other scores over fifty, so that his Sunday afternoon average was a fraction under 60.

Essentially, however, it was farewell. Wayne has always had a healthy attitude to the problems of how a player fits into a team and how to respond to difficult situations. Asked how he felt when a younger player appeared in the team and threatened to displace an established man – and in 1991 Alan Fordham and Nigel Felton were doing precisely that to Wayne – he replied: 'Well, if he does better than me, that's it. I've got to try and do better than him. I am not going to stay awake at night because a nineteen-year-old might take my place.' A far cry from the *Botham Report,* where Ian explains that many modern players are so fearful of losing

Wayne batting for Northants at the end of his career with the County Club. (David Munden)

Northamptonshire versus Warwickshire at Edgbaston in September 1991. Dicky Bird signals five runs as the ball strikes the helmet. Wayne, in trendy shoes and flared trousers, surveys the incident from his usual position at first slip. Andy Roberts is the bowler, Wayne Noon the wicketkeeper and Rob Bailey is at point. (David Capel)

their place in a county side that they go to desperate lengths to cover up an injury, the most common device being the use of anti-inflammatory drugs. Wayne has also taken the same resigned view of poor umpiring decisions: 'If you get a bad decision, you've got to hold your head up high, stick your chest out, have a few beers and get stuck in again in the morning.'

Many people were sad when Wayne left Wantage Road. He had been with the County for twenty-three years, but with the chance to move away from Northampton after the break-up of his marriage, the prospect of a four-year contract and greater financial security with Durham and, in addition, the prospect of a second benefit or testimonial, the whole package seemed to make sense. David Capel, who had first come to the County in 1981 and had shared many experiences with Wayne at both County and Test level, was perhaps the one who regretted Wayne's departure most. 'Ned was such a colourful character, such superb company and on the day he left there was a lot taken away from the Club.' David enjoyed Wayne's buccaneering spirit, his determination to win matches for the benefit of the team, whatever the cost in personal success. Much of Wayne's way of looking at cricket rubbed off on David and, now that he has retired from the first-class game himself, David is enjoying his post of director of excellence with the youth squads, precisely the lads who worshipped Wayne when he was at the Club.

When the time to go came, Wayne had played 363 first-class matches for

Northamptonshire. He had batted on 628 occasions, had been not out in only 43 (an opener's burden when it comes to averages) and scored 20,317 runs at an average of 34.73. He had struck 44 hundreds, three of them double tons, and had also taken 40 wickets. Many pundits assert that a batting average in the region of 40 runs per innings is necessary to qualify for top-class status and, although a case can be made for this argument, it takes no account of how many innings a batsman plays which actually win matches. Here Wayne enjoys a quite enviable record. Furthermore, the first-class game is not the only thing, especially nowadays. Only Alistair Brown (203), Graham Gooch (176) and Ian Botham (175 not out) have exceeded Wayne's great Sunday afternoon knock of 172 not out. And his 158 came pretty close, too. It wasn't a bad record to go away with.

Wayne tries his hand as a model at a fashion show in Northampton in 1991. (John Courtney)

16

SECOND INNINGS AT DURHAM

County Durham has always enjoyed a good standard of cricket. In the early 1880s, a county club of sorts had been founded which was based on South Shields Cricket Club. In 1895 this club attempted to become a Minor County and, although progress stuttered a little in the opening years, Durham was finally confirmed as such in 1899, from which time it continued until 1991. It enjoyed some success in the inter-war years, but it was not until the 1970s that things really began to take off. Between August 1976, when the Club lost to Northumberland, and August 1982, when Staffordshire defeated them, they went through a period of sixty-five Minor County matches without defeat, a record which still stands. They won the Minor Counties Championship in 1976, 1980, 1981 and 1984, were runners-up three times in the late seventies and, when they left the scene in 1991, their record had not been bettered by any other Minor County. Only Buckinghamshire's nine championships equalled them.

When they had met first-class counties they had also made their mark. They were among the first Minor Counties to join the Gillette Cup in 1964, and in 1973 they defeated a Yorkshire side, captained by Geoffrey Boycott and containing six Test players, by five wickets. They were the first Minor County to defeat a first-class side in this competition and, when it became the Natwest Trophy, Durham were again the first to defeat a senior side, this time Derbyshire by seven wickets in 1985. Their opponents on this occasion fielded none other than West Indian fast-bowling legend, Michael Holding.

Durham had kept themselves in cricket's public eye in two other ways. Over the years the County had established a tradition of always being pleased to entertain visiting overseas sides, the last occasion being the visit of the Victorian state side in 1991, when home-grown product John Glendenen scored 200, the first double hundred by a Durham player for eighty-five years. The second feature was the emergence of Durham University as a centre of cricketing excellence which has made a forceful mark on what was the Universities Athletic Union Championship. They remain just as successful in the British University Sports Association Championship, now generously sponsored by the Halifax Bank. Durham has certainly challenged Oxford and Cambridge Universities as a breeding ground for first-class cricketers and has produced many county players and five Test players: Paul Allott, Tim Curtis, Graeme Fowler (now the University's director of excellence), Nasser Hussain and John Stephenson.

The last county to join the English County Championship was Glamorgan in 1921. Buckinghamshire had been invited at the same time but, perhaps strangely, had declined. Nothing had disturbed the quiet flow of the Championship until the 1980s, when Northumberland and Shropshire had flirted with applications, but both counties had finally withdrawn. The idea of Durham's making an application started at a committee meeting in 1988 and gathered momentum apace. An application to the TCCB in 1989 was followed by an acceptance in principle at the end of 1990. One of the driving forces behind the application was Don Robson, who had been Chairman of the Durham Cricket

Wayne as Durham CCC opening batsman. (David Munden)

Wayne, now Durham's opening batsman, drives on the off-side. (David Munden)

Association and Leader of Durham County Council. He would eventually become Chairman of the County Cricket Club. The reasons for the County's successful application centred on the strength of cricket in the area, the nine major leagues which attracted well-known overseas players as professionals and the fact that, unlike a county such as Berkshire that might be seen to be muscling in on the territory of established counties, Durham would be extending the frontiers of first-class cricket. Grounds on which to play abounded: Durham University, Stockton-on-Tees, Darlington, Hartlepool, Gateshead Fell, and Chester-le-Street. Furthermore, there were plans to build an entirely new ground at Riverside, Chester-le-Street, which actually came into use in 1995, but where the wicket has had troubles exceeding that which might be described as 'teething'.

Geoff Cook's task as Director of Cricket was to recruit talent carefully and diplomatically, both from among local players and sources further afield. David Graveney, now England's Chairman of Selectors and Secretary of the Professional Cricketers' Association, became the first captain. Funnily enough, he had been captain of Gloucestershire in the years 1981 to 1988, exactly the same period, therefore, when Geoff had been leading Northants. Connections with Victoria in Australia led to the recruitment of Dean Jones, a batsman of immense ability, whose Test career had been curtailed by his inability to come to terms with Bobby Simpson, the Australian manager. But perhaps the biggest coup of all was the signing of Ian Botham, who had left Somerset in high dudgeon, had helped Worcestershire to some success and now relished the prospect of a club close to his North Yorkshire home near Richmond. Wayne was an obvious choice too, given his connections with Geoff Cook, and other players, such as Paul Parker from Sussex, John Morris from Derbyshire, Simon Hughes from Middlesex and Phil Bainbridge from Gloucestershire, all jocularly named the

Wayne outside the Dun Cow public house, next to his home in Sedgefield.

'cavaliers', joined the local players to form a competitive nucleus.

Wayne and Debbie and her two daughters set off, therefore, from their romantic cottage in Kingsthorp and settled in a rented house in Fore Street, Sedgefield, which was conveniently next door to the Dun Cow pub and overlooked the racecourse, both major plus factors as far as Wayne was concerned. He earned much respect and affection from Durham cricket *aficionados* by positively taking up residence in the county. David Graveney, the skipper, lived in the Marriott Hotel in Gateshead throughout his tenancy of the post, while Ian Botham relished being in his country estate more often, with its boating lake, and others merely took temporary accommodation. Wayne has always been a good mixer and he soon became a firm favourite with the supporters in much the same way that he had been at Wantage Road. Richard Peel comments from his days at the *Chronicle & Echo* in Northampton how well Wayne always responded to requests for autographs and how well he understood his obligations as a player when it came to keeping cricket supporters happy. He was always ready to sit, talk and joke with people in the pavilion and he certainly continued in this vein when he arrived at Durham.

Back at Northampton, however, things were less bright. Dolphin Cottage, on the green at Kingsthorp, had been empty since Wayne and Debbie moved to Sedgefield and they were unable to keep up the mortgage payments on the £150,000 property. This led to the Abbey National Bank's repossessing the cottage in a case in the county court, where they also sought to declare Wayne bankrupt. It was not the best start to a new career in the North East, but Wayne has a fairly tight defence when he is on the back foot. 'It's happening to people in all walks of life,' he nonchalantly told Newcastle's *Sunday Sun*.

When the 1992 season began there was no question of Wayne's wondering whether he would claim an opening spot. It was never in doubt and he had the pleasure of taking the first ball bowled to Durham as a first-class county when they faced Leicestershire on the University ground at the end of April. Although success eluded him in this match, it was not long before Wayne was back to his old form. Cardiff had always been one of his happy hunting grounds and, batting in what the *Times* described as his 'old buccaneering style', he hammered a powerful 143, including seventeen boundaries, off the Glamorgan attack. Simon Hughes, writing in *From Minor to Major* described Wayne's innings as 'scintillating', but added: 'I must say he has the most laid-back approach of anyone I know, even Botham. He arrived this morning at ten past ten, carrying only with essential equipment – a bottle of shampoo and twenty Benson & Hedges. He did not deign to do the warm-ups but then sat in a cloud of nicotine until eleven o'clock after which he pummelled the bowling to all parts.' This innings was his fiftieth first-class century. In conjunction with Dean Jones he added 206 for the second wicket and, when Paul Parker contributed his third ton in six innings, the fledgling county declared on a massive 521 for 9 wickets. Glamorgan's first innings of 224 had been modest and their second knock was even more so, registering a mere 193, of which Tony Cottey contributed a brave 112 not out. Viv Richards, now with his second English county, contributed 8 runs in two attempts and Durham romped home for their first Championship victory by an innings and 104 runs.

Wayne continued with a string of good scores and, when the Pakistan touring team arrived at Chester-le-Street in early July in good form after squaring the Test series by beating England at Lord's, Wayne scored a rapid 118 in a partnership of 162 with Dean Jones in only 28 overs. Durham had begun their first-class career by playing Leicestershire and at the end of July it was time for the return match. Durham were bowled out for 145 early on the second morning after a frustrating first day when play did not begin until

4.00 p.m. The hosts responded boldly and took a lead of 111 just before the close on the second evening. Wayne and Stewart Hutton had a few difficult overs to face in the growing gloom. Hutton departed quickly, caught off pace-bowler David Millns, who was roaring down the hill at the Grace Road end and Simon Hughes was sent in as nightwatchman. He tells a most amusing story in his book *A Lot of Hard Yakka*.

> *Millns took an early wicket and, with five minutes to go, tore at Larkins. The first two deliveries fizzed close to his jaw and thwacked into the 'keeper's gloves, still rising. I, the nightwatchman, stood quaking in my boots at the other end. The third was another flesh-seeking lifter. Larkins swayed back and thrashed it past cover. The fourth spat from a length and nearly took his hand off; the fifth grazed his right shoulder. Certain he had Larkins for the taking, Millns sought a fuller length with the last, expecting a rattle of furniture. Larkins launched it through the covers and into the boundary boards with such force it rebounded back to the bowler. Walking up the wicket at the end of the over in shock, I expected some adrenaline-induced comment or morsel of advice. All he grunted was 'Piece of piss' and walked back.*

What Simon Hughes does not record is perhaps typical of Wayne Larkins. Next morning he was out, caught Benson bowled Millns, for eight. Panache does not always produce rewards.

Wayne sailed though the rest of his first Durham season. When the return match with Glamorgan took place at Hartlepool in August he rubbed salt in the visitors' May-time wounds and led his county's second innings with 140, which contained 5 sixes and 19 fours, 76 per cent of his score in boundaries. Later in the season, despite a bad blow on the hamstring which necessitated his having a runner, wholly out of keeping with the macho Larkins, he made up for a first innings duck against Somerset with a solid 117. It

Desert Orchid with Wayne at the opening of the tote in Sedgefield.

was a good innings because Andy Caddick, Somerset's pace-man, was anxious to impress the England selectors, and had been on top form and had battered Wayne black and blue by the end of his stay at the crease.

At the end of the season Wayne had scored 1,417 Championship runs and had played in twenty-one of the twenty-two games, in both instances more than any other Durham player. Including his knock against the Pakistanis, he had topped 1,500 runs for the season and made 4 hundreds, which replicated the form he showed for Northants in his glory days. Despite Wayne's efforts, Durham's fortunes in the Championship were less happy. They recorded only two wins and finished at the bottom of the table. On the other hand, their form in one-day competitions, where Wayne's contributions were sound rather than outstanding, achieved much more and they ended in a creditable eighth equal place in the Sunday League. Durham had, at least, got their foot in the door.

In October, at the end of his first season, Wayne joined a touring party, led by Mike Brearley, on an expenses only trip to Barbados to play two charity matches for a so-called Masters' Over 35's side against a similar West Indian team captained by Clive Lloyd. Here he almost met with a fatal accident. He and Debbie had just had supper at the Bamboo Beach Bar in Bridgetown and were walking back to the Beach Village Hotel in what they believed to be the exclusive district of St James. Suddenly a mugger with a knife leapt out at Wayne, cut his head and then stabbed him in the side. Luckily, Wayne was able to strike back and the man staggered and ran off. Wayne took it with great equanimity – after all, here was a man who had faced some of the world's fastest bowlers – and walked back to the hotel. When he arrived there, blood was pouring from the wound and the hotel manager fainted. The staff called an ambulance and Wayne landed up in hospital and required twenty stitches to his side. He was, however, soon out of hospital, but he missed his two matches. Watching the team practise, he told the press: 'It was a bad experience, but I won't say any more.' Mike Brearley, his tour skipper, was amazed at Wayne's calmness. 'I can recall that he seemed entirely without malice or resentment. Few other people would have been.'

Wayne had three more seasons with his adopted county before his controversial dismissal at the end of the 1995 season. In those three seasons, Durham continued to struggle in the County Championship, finishing bottom again in 1993, two places up to sixteenth in 1994 and saved from the wooden spoon in 1995 only by tons by Wayne and John Morris in the final match against Nottinghamshire. It was at the conclusion of this match that Wayne was ushered with undue haste into the cricketers' departure lounge. Thankfully for the new county, they fared rather better in one-day encounters and, although they made little progress in either the Natwest Trophy or the Benson & Hedges Cup, their Sunday afternoon performances kept them mainly in the middle of the table.

In 1993 Wayne enjoyed almost as good a season as he had done in his first year at Durham. He scored Championship tons against Sussex and Warwickshire and managed 5 fifties, but he was forced to endure some dull batting by Hampshire in the rain affected match at Stockton-on-Tees in May, which *Wisden* described as 'hardly likely to set the pulse racing.' Tony Middleton and Paul Terry ground out an opening stand of 134 on the seaming wicket and, before the weather had a merciful final say, Terry completed his hundred in 373 minutes. Graeme Fowler, another of the former Test and county batsmen whom Durham initially recruited, was standing at slip with Wayne and noticed that he was becoming irritated, even angry, at the proceedings. He quizzed Wayne on the cause of his annoyance only to receive the reply: 'Who wants to watch this? He's ruining the game. I couldn't play like this, could you? You must keep the game going forward.' This, of course, was typical Wayne Larkins' philosophy of cricket. Play positive cricket and look for chances to win a match, rather than merely draw it. 'I don't care if it's one-day or five-day, the first five overs or the last five, if I see a bad ball I'll go out and whack it.'

The Australians were the summer visitors in 1993 and in July they came up to the University ground to play Durham. Wayne had a marvellous opportunity to put his philosophy into practice. The Australians had always thought that Wayne had been under-used by England at the top of his career and they were soon to see some evidence of this. David Graveney won the toss and batted. Wayne put on 91 for the first wicket with Graeme Fowler and then went on to a magnificent 151, with all but 31 of these runs coming by way of 27 fours and 2 sixes. John Parker, writing in the *Sunday Times* was almost fulsome in his praise. 'Larkins, at his best, is still one of the most attractive batsmen in the country. He drives through the ball on the walk as though hitting fours is the natural role of batting.' It was not as if the Australians had put out a weak side. Led by Allan Border, the team contained seven players who would help to defeat England by an innings in the Fourth Test at Leeds in the following week. At one stage the visitors were 113 for 7 wickets in their first innings, but they recovered to secure a draw as a result of second innings tons by Matthew Hayden and David Boon after their side had been forced to follow on. Wayne and the Durham team had given them one hell of a fright and it was just a pity that England capitulated so easily at Headingley against virtually the same team.

In the spring of 1994 Wayne and Debbie were invited by the Barbados Tourist Board to visit the island as a form of recompense for the mugging and stabbing which Wayne had endured some eighteen months previously. It was certainly a kind and generous gesture. Unfortunately Wayne allowed himself to be interviewed by the *News of the World* prior to their flying out to the Caribbean. What is worse, he found himself, so he now asserts, misquoted. The bold banner headline read 'King Cons!' It referred, of course, to the occasion in Trinidad in 1990 when the West Indies team under Desmond Haynes, facing defeat by England, bowled only 17 overs in the final two hours. 'Forget Pakistan,' Wayne is reported as saying. 'For cold-blooded, cynical, calculating gamesmanship there is nobody to touch the Windies!' The remarks were styled as advice to Michael Atherton and his team who were touring West Indies at this time, but it went badly wrong and Wayne was highly embarrassed by his indiscretion.

The 1994 season started well enough for Wayne. He played his highest innings for Durham when he made 158 not out in a win against Gloucestershire at Gateshead Fell at the end of May. It was a grassy wicket and ideally suited to the visitors' overseas player, West Indian Courtney Walsh, whose opening spell caused chaos at the top of the Durham order. In the end Wayne secured some dominance over Walsh and, of his 28 fours, seven were taken off the West Indian. As the *Daily Telegraph* reporter noted: 'His timing, always a hallmark of his batting, was in exquisitely good order. His superbly timed and placed front-foot drives brought him 17 fours in an arc between mid-on and cover as well as a straight six.' This tremendous innings, lasting five-and-a-half hours, the first case of a Durham player carrying his bat, comprised much of the County's 305 because the next highest score was 31 extras. Geoff Cook was equally ecstatic at his former partner's efforts. 'I've known him for twenty-four years,' he told the press, 'and I rate that knock among his top five.'

The County travelled south after their win and visited Edgbaston to play Warwickshire. They must have felt that they were on something of a roll as, thanks to John Morris' 204, they declared at 556 for 8 wickets. Little did anyone know what was to follow. At the end of the second day the hosts had reached 210 for 2 wickets with Brian Lara, dropped by wicketkeeper Chris Scott when his score was only 20, on 111 not out. After a day off owing to rain Wayne, in his usual position at first slip, had a grandstand view of Lara's historic 501 not out.

There were, however, the signs of chinks in Wayne's armour. He was constantly being struck on the hands. Allan Donald caused him to retire hurt off the first ball of the match when the County entertained the South African tourists at Chester-le-Street in July and, at the beginning of August in the match with Somerset at Taunton, Adrianus van Troost, the home county's Dutch pace-bowler, fractured Wayne's wrist. Out for much of the rest of the season, he failed to complete his 1,000 runs but still managed to average over 40 runs per innings.

Times when he was not on the cricket field were for Wayne at this stage of his career really quite pleasant. He enjoyed living near Sedgefield Racecourse as he had always taken an interest in the turf. After all, a projected visit to the races at Worcester had significantly altered his personal life. And the golf was good as well. Like most able cricketers he had considerable talent on a golf course. Wayne's four-year contract with Durham brought in for a summer's work as much as many people earn in a year and, together with Debbie's own job, they were able to live a comfortable, but not extravagant, life despite their problems with Dolphin Cottage.

Wayne set out, therefore, on his 1995 season, the last of his contract, with a reasonable belief that he would be re-engaged and might look forward to some form of benefit or testimonial. The season started modestly, but at the beginning of June he found himself relegated to the middle order. Durham's new skipper, Mike Roseberry, the son of Matty Roseberry, a Durham CCC Board member, had come up from Middlesex and was an accredited opening batsman. To compound the problem, Wayne suffered yet another injury. In the Sunday League match with Essex at Chelmsford he managed to get his thumb broken again. This meant his absence for much of June and July and it was not until the game with Northants at Wantage Road in August that he found himself back in the side. This was another of Durham's disaster matches – they recorded thirteen losses out of seventeen matches during the season – and it was also the turning point in Wayne's relations with the County. Bowled out for 148 in their first innings, Durham were unable to restrict their hosts' batting and Northants declared on 492 for 5 wickets. Although Wayne and Stewart Hutton added 181 for the first wicket, the innings closed on 268, a loss by an innings and 76 runs. But there was a silver lining: Wayne, in scoring 112, had completed his 'full set', that is to say, a hundred against every county in the Championship, an achievement not to be sniffed at. Everyone was delighted, nobody more than Wayne. 'I still relish the challenge. I hope it showed out here. It was particularly nice to complete the full set at Wantage Road,' he told the waiting reporters. Of course, Wayne celebrated in full, as only he knows how, throughout the evening and into Sunday. In the morning he drove to Roxton to pick up his mother to bring her to watch the Sunday League match. When he appeared in the dressing room at the start of the match, he was found to be in no fit condition to play a game of cricket and was replaced by Jon Longley. There was outrage on the part of Don Robson, the Durham Chairman. How could a senior player be so far under the influence that he could not play cricket? Wayne asserted that he had been able in the morning to drive to Roxton to collect his mother: why was there a problem? A small cricketing one for sure, a greater motoring one perhaps. It was a misfortune, too, for Mavis Larkins who had come to watch Wayne perform – after all, now that he had moved to Durham her chances had been severely restricted – and she had always been such an enthusiastic supporter both of her son and of Northamptonshire cricket.

The season moved on. Little more was said and no fines were imposed, but there must have been thoughts amongst Board members. In the last Championship match of the season Durham were to play Nottinghamshire at the new Riverside Ground. If they won, they would avoid the wooden spoon and Kent would be consigned to last place. If they lost, they would finish bottom for the third year out of their first four as a first-class county. Wayne, with 121, his tenth ton for the County, and John Morris with 109 ensured a commanding total of 424. Nottinghamshire were no match for their hosts, followed on and were beaten by an innings. The wooden spoon was avoided.

Wayne clearly felt that a renewal of his contract was just a formality. So did the dressing room. As the players left the field, however, at the end of the Nottinghamshire innings Geoff Cook had in what he described later as 'the hardest decision of my life' to tell Wayne that he was not being retained by Durham. A little later Geoff came to the portacabin, which served as a press room at the Riverside ground, to give the news to the media. 'Wayne Larkins is being released by Durham County Cricket Club. Please do not ask me to justify this decision' is virtually all he said. It was incredibly sad and traumatic for both parties. After all, they had been good mates as well as a famous opening pair at Northampton and had drunk more than just the one pint together after matches. 'Et tu, Brute?' could perhaps have been uttered.

Wayne was asked to play in the Sunday League game which followed the Championship match, but declined. The whole affair had been appallingly handled. No one said goodbye; Wayne had to go back to Sedgefield to tell Debbie that he had been sacked and there was a dreadful scene in the sponsors' lounge after the Sunday League match. Geoff Cook had had the courage to turn up, but there was something more than frostiness between the two former openers. Wayne lost his cool, probably for the first time in his life, called for Don Robson, who apparently had not arrived, and told the press to naff off. Mike Roseberry did his best to defuse the situation, but it was a wholly embarrassing and regrettable occasion.

There are, however, many other factors to be considered. The accepted wisdom is that Durham CCC were bad handlers of men. Mike Roseberry, Graeme Fowler and John Morris, to name only three, felt that the County had undervalued them and Ian Botham has subsequently said that joining Durham was the worst decision that he ever made in his career. There was also confusion about the strength of Durham's batting for the 1996 season. They had every hope of re-engaging Dean Jones, but when he was offered the captaincy at Derbyshire as well as a lucrative contract, he spurned Durham and opted for the Midland county. Had this been known a little earlier, Wayne might just have survived. He had to contend, however, with an attempt by the Durham establishment to impose a pattern of discipline. More was to follow. At the end of the 1996 season, for instance, Darren Blenkiron, who had scored two Championship centuries, was summarily dismissed for damaging two club cars after a night out. And then, finally, there was the question of Wayne's own form. An average for the season of 32 was barely enough, and Geoff Cook had apparently noted slippages in his game, even failings in technique. He often seemed to get hit on the head and possibly he was seen as belonging to another era in which efficiency was not quite so important. What is more, the pitches at the new Riverside ground did not help any batsman. It was opened at least a year too early owing to pressures from sponsors and the wicket was below the watertable of the River Wear. The location was, therefore, generally poor, despite the fact that the ground was visually stunning. Although the manner of Wayne's dismissal was brutal in the extreme it might be said that another short contract would only have been delaying the inevitable. For all that, Wayne had been promised a benefit, but was overlooked, while Phil Bainbridge was lucky enough to be awarded a testimonial.

Nobody can doubt that Wayne had served Durham pretty well. Yes, it is true that he had

Wayne, Debbie and her two daughters stay at Sandy Beach Hotel as guests of the Barbados Tourist Board.

created an image of being laid back, the player with a fag in his mouth and the chunky Stuart Surridge bat at the ready. While most players preferred to use their favourite bats from whatever supplier and disguise them with their sponsor's stickers, Wayne never bothered to engage in such a subterfuge but just used the bat Stuart Surridge supplied for him. There was an impression that both he and Ian Botham had taken life at Durham quite casually despite their abundant talent. Certainly they liked to spend their time first thing in the morning potting cricket balls around the outfield with their bats instead of joining in the warm-ups or having throw-downs. But Wayne had been idolised by the youngsters at Durham and had never complained about anything – injury, batting in the gloaming, poor wickets, even bad umpiring decisions. And, sometimes, figures do speak. He scored over 4,300 first-class runs for Durham at an average of nearly 38 – higher than that he achieved at Northampton – and recorded 10 hundreds and 20 fifties. At one-day level, too, his record stands examination: 2,300 runs, also at an average of nearly 38, with 7 tons and 9 fifties. Throw in over 60 catches at first slip, including seven in the match against Somerset at Chester-le-Street in his final season, and Durham can certainly be said to have had their money's worth out of Wayne Larkins.

Cricket normally finds ways of reconciliation and, thankfully, a chance to bury the hatchet appeared in this case too. Wayne was invited back to Chester-le-Street to accept honorary life membership of Durham County Cricket Club and he accepted with grace, but not before saying: 'After twenty-six years in the game, it wasn't the end of my career that I had planned. Leaving the game without much dignity, without much pride – it hurt. It left a bit of a scar.' Don Robson was keen to put the matter right: 'Wayne did a hell of a job for us. Whatever he does and wherever he goes, Wayne Larkins will always be welcome at this Club.' This is only how it should be, but there was one thing nobody else had thought much about – a gaping hole in the Larkins' budget.

17
BACK TO HIS ROOTS

The fact that Wayne had not been retained by Durham caused a certain surprise among most cricket fans through England, but primarily, of course, it came as a shock to Wayne and Debbie. On the day of fateful news, when Geoff Cook had announced the County's decision, he went back to a sad and tearful house at Sedgefield. Apart from the unexpected nature of the news and the sense of loss of pride and dignity, there was also a financial implication. The loss of a £30,000 salary would put a dent into the budget of most families and this was true in Wayne's case. He began to think about how it all happened. 'A lot of it is my own fault,' he later told Tim Rich of the *Newcastle Chronicle & Journal*, 'I should have organised myself better. My biggest mistake was relying on my income from cricket which I thought would never end. I'd seen it happen to others, but you kid yourself it isn't going to happen to you.'

Wayne had to take some immediate remedial action and it was his good fortune that Richmondshire, a club playing in the North Yorkshire/South Durham League, was hunting for a professional. His first step, therefore, was to sign for this local club and, as a bonus, they told him that they wanted him to captain the side. The second avenue came through Mike Green, now Bedfordshire's membership secretary. Since the day when Wayne, as a fourteen-year-old, had batted with Mike and won the game for Bedford Town Second XI at Winchmore Hill he had always kept in touch with Wayne. When Mike heard that he was on the market he immediately rang him and asked him to consider playing Minor Counties cricket. This was something that Wayne had never done or known much about, simply because he had gone to Northamptonshire as a professional at the age of fifteen. The Bedfordshire Committee were, of course, keen to have an ex-England player joining their ranks as a professional, especially because Wayne had been born in the county. Wayne felt that he needed to think the matter over, but when Mike, joined by Barry Robinson, Bedfordshire's Chairman, and David Hoare, the Club Secretary, took the trouble to come up to Sedgefield to see him, he did not need much convincing to accept a contract for the 1996 season. There had been, however, two things he had needed to consider. The first was that he had been unsure about the nature of Minor Counties cricket. He had thought that it might be merely a stepping stone for younger players to go on and play the first-class game. He soon found out that its standard was a good deal higher than that of county second elevens and this had helped him to make a decision. The second point he had thought about was the amount of travelling between Sedgefield, where his Saturday commitments with Richmondshire necessarily kept him till late in the day, and the venues of Bedfordshire's matches which were usually played on a Sunday and a Monday. It was not that easy, but one thing a professional cricketer soon learns is that you have to be prepared to spend a fair time behind the wheel of your car.

Wayne's first season with Bedfordshire was one of incredible and record-breaking success, although he caused some flutters before his first match against Lincolnshire at Sleaford. It was known that Wayne would need to travel on the Saturday evening the 150-odd miles from his game with Richmondshire to Sleaford, and the Bedfordshire team expected him at about 11.00 p.m. When it came to midnight and there was still no

Wayne, people at the team hotel began to get worried. 'We did tell him that he was being picked for this game, didn't we?' 'Oh, yes, he knows all right.' Most players wanted to get off to bed, but Mike Green agreed to wait up for Wayne He had a long wait. At 3.00 a.m. on the Sunday Wayne, true to his eccentric time-keeping, arrived totally unconcerned at the hotel. 'I needed a swift half after the Richmondshire game. Sorry I'm a bit late.'

It was all worth it. Although Wayne did not prosper in his first innings for his new team, he rattled up 124 in the second knock. David Hoare recalls how Wayne's pride has never left him. Tapping the Bedfordshire logo on his sweater and grinning through his moustache, he said after his 124: 'My first hundred for my native county.' This hundred was followed by 129 in the MCC Trophy competition against Oxfordshire, which Bedfordshire won easily, and then by 101 not out against Suffolk, where he enjoyed playing against his former Test colleague, Derek Randall, and matching him with his ability as a fielder. In July Wayne opened the innings against Northumberland with the then seventeen-year-old Graeme Swann, who is now a professional with Northamptonshire and part of England's plans for the future. It caused great amusement among the Bedfordshire side when Graeme started to outscore the maestro of the 'Nedding' treatment to such an extent that, when the first wicket fell at 130 and Graeme departed for 76, Wayne's score had not yet reached 40. As the match report says: 'He watched admiringly from the other end with the air of someone who has seen it all before.' Of course, he himself went on to 118 not out from Bedfordshire's declared total of 253 for 2 wickets. His success continued. There was in mid-season a massive 155 not out against Buckinghamshire in the fourth innings to win the match for his side by five wickets, reminiscent, of course, of those Northants fourth innings run chases. With 109 against Cambridgeshire and another 101 not out against Cumberland, Wayne enjoyed a marvellous season of 1,024 runs with 6 hundreds and 2 fifties at an average of over 73. The only disappointment was that, in the MCC Trophy final at Lord's at the end of August, Bedfordshire were beaten by Cheshire by five wickets.

There was one irony that was not lost on Wayne at the end of the 1996 season. Durham failed to win a match in the County Championship and finished, predictably, in last place, as they also did in the Sunday League, where they managed just one win, against Essex, to compensate for fifteen losses. A second round exit from the Natwest Trophy and being the only team above the Minor Counties in their Benson & Hedges group made for a dreadful season. Dean Jones had led Derbyshire to second place in the County Championship and Wayne had been the backbone of his native county. If he had been of a vindictive nature Wayne would have laughed heartily, but that would be uncharacteristic. However, Philip Hoare, Bedfordshire's captain in 1996, did indicate in his annual report just how influential Wayne had been: 'His presence both on and off the field was an inspiration to all. He is one of the most genuine people you could ever meet and he immediately became 'one of the team', which is not always the case with some ex-first-class players.' Wayne's influence on Bedfordshire's affairs continued to be felt in the 1997 season. The County won the Eastern Division of the Championship and narrowly lost, on run-rate, the play-off with Devonshire, the Western Division winners. Wayne's own contribution, if slightly less dramatic than that of the previous season, was still imposing, with over 850 runs – more than any other Minor Counties batsman – plus 3 hundreds and 7 fifties at an average of over 50.

Before the start of the next season, Wayne received news that both shocked and saddened him. In the first week of January 1998, David 'Bluey' Bairstow, Yorkshire's former wicketkeeper and captain, was found hanged in his home at Marton-cum-Grafton in North Yorkshire. He was only forty-six. He had made his debut for Yorkshire in 1970, when still at school. Needing to take his A-level English Literature on the second day of the match, he sat the examination by special arrangement at 7.00 a.m. before setting off to Bradford Park Avenue to play against Gloucestershire. Subsequently he played for his county for twenty years and in four Test matches and twenty-one one-day internationals for England. Wayne had got to know him well both on and off the field on the county circuit and, later on, when they had been together on Over 35's unofficial overseas tours. David was experiencing problems with his second marriage, his promotional company was in difficulties and there was a drink-driving charge pending. Furthermore there was a distinct cashflow problem. It was rather unnerving, as some of David's problems resembled Wayne's.

The fact that an ex-professional cricketer had come upon hard times and had taken his life was picked up with alacrity by the media. Wayne received an approach in May from David Norrie, the biographer of Michael Atherton and a sports journalist with the *News of the World,* who invited him to be the subject of an article. It appeared under the banner headline: 'I won't survive another winter.' Whether this was a wise move on Wayne's part was open to doubt, but it did show the shattering effect of a cricket professional being suddenly dismissed with no opportunity to make provision for his future career. In the article Wayne outlined how he felt about life after Durham. Because he had been so successful, from a cricketing point of view, in taking on a contract with Bedfordshire, his parlous financial position had not come to the forefront. Wayne pointed out in the article how money problems undermine the whole basis of one's life and can lead to domestic turmoil. People find it hard to believe that an international cricketer who has had a benefit with a county has not got some money stashed away. In Wayne's case the profit was from his ill-fated rebel tour and his benefit went mainly into the Hardingstone house which, when he left his family, he handed over in total to Jane. At this time

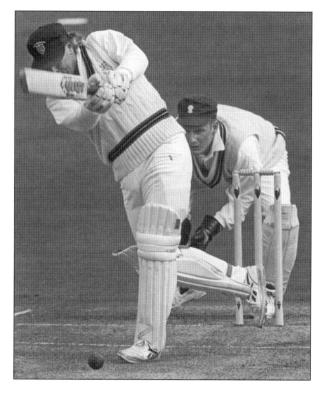

Wayne batting for Bedfordshire CCC against Cheshire CCC in the Minor Counties' Final at Lord's in August 1996. (Bill Smith)

Bedfordshire CCC, winners of the ECB Thirty-eight-county competition against Cumberland CCC, at Lord's in September 1999. Wayne is seated second from left. (Bill Smith)

he felt particularly aggrieved that, while he accepted that his own behaviour had contributed largely to the marital breakdown, Jane kept coming back for more. He was now making less than £10,000 a year between April and September from his Bedfordshire contract and from playing as a professional for Sedgefield (his post with Richmondshire having disappeared when the club was relegated in the league and no longer able to employ a professional). There was bound to be some shortfall after having earned £30,000 a year at Durham, but his maintenance contributions remained the same, £600 per month. If he ever fell behind with them, then he was likely to land up in court and, being unable to afford a solicitor, was forced to represent himself. 'They make me look a mug,' he mentioned in the interview, 'it's so embarrassing.'

Bedfordshire did not achieve any trophies in the 1998 season when Wayne's own contribution also fell off. Some 400 runs at an average of 27 was well below the achievements of his first two seasons with the County and 1999 did not show any improvement, although Bedfordshire won the MCC Trophy at Lord's when they beat Cumberland in September.

In 1998 Wayne and Debbie moved from Sedgefield and settled in Leamington Spa, where Debbie's job now took her. Wayne has been able to play as a professional for the Leamington Spa Club and has scored well for them, but he has actively sought other employment as well. At one time he entertained the idea of becoming an umpire. After all, his two former Northampton colleagues, Peter Willey and George Sharp, had done just that and not only were they on the English first-class list but they had done well enough to be appointed to the international panel, which meant winter work and travel as well. Asked one day whether he enjoyed umpiring, Peter replied jocularly: 'Beats work any time.' Wayne has, however, been unable to grasp the nettle of this style of work and, although everyone, not least Audrey Hoare, the wife of Bedfordshire's secretary, has commented how well Wayne is able to deal with younger players and encourage them, he has not been able to find a school or other coaching appointment. For the present he asserts cheerfully: 'I enjoy playing cricket hugely and I'll carry on as long as I can and people want me.'

Sadly, time waits for no man.

AFTERWORD

If, as Richard Peel, once a Northampton journalist and now ITV's Director of Public Relations, has suggested – and there is much more to say for his argument than against it – Wayne Larkins was the greatest English batsman since the Second World War not to have achieved a proper international career, how is it possible for such a situation to have come about? Can talent in any area of our sporting life be so easily squandered? It is clear that it can be, so what significant reasons for this failure need to be identified?

Britain has for too long in its history prided itself on the fact that the expert must always be 'on tap', but never 'on top'. The amateur, the man who can distance himself from the point at issue and take a supposedly dispassionate view of things, has constantly been allowed to infiltrate and run our national institutions – and Test cricket is certainly one of these! For several years after 1945 every commanding height of cricket was in the hands of amateurs, often reasonable and pleasant men in every respect, but men with interests which lay beyond cricket. It represented a massive turn-around when the professional Len Hutton was appointed Test captain in 1952. He succeeded against India, won back the Ashes in 1953 and a series against Pakistan was drawn. For some of hierarchy in the world of cricket this was apparently not good enough. When it came to his taking our Test side to Australia for the 1954/55 series, there was some suspicion about a professional captain, and many voices called for the Reverend David Sheppard to be appointed in his stead. There was certainly nothing wrong with David Sheppard as a man – and his cricket was pretty good too – but his main ambition in life was the Church and how well he fulfilled that calling. He was an amateur cricketer in the best sense. Len Hutton's successor was Peter May, another marvellous batsman and astute captain, but also an amateur, who finally became an insurance broker. There is nothing wrong with that either. But what was wrong was a culture of amateurism and, even though amateur status disappeared in 1962, the culture lived on. Brian Close enjoyed a short spell in charge in 1966 and 1967, but he then fell foul of the establishment and it was not until 1969, when Raymond Illingworth was appointed to the captaincy, that a professional in the truest sense was given a good run at the job. Selection, however, was in the hands of the great and the good at Lord's and their backgrounds were essentially 'amateur'. While, therefore, it was true that Test captains from the time of the abolition of amateur status were 'cricketers' and not amateurs, they were appointed by selection committees who largely had a master and servant outlook towards professional cricketers. One chairman of selectors even referred to Malcolm Devon, when he meant Devon Malcolm. If you don't know the names of your team you are hardly likely to understand them as men. There are many reasons why England's cricket has declined in relation to other Test-playing nations over the last forty years, but one that is of the greatest importance is clearly how Test match sides are selected and trained. For much of the period in question there have been seventeen first-class counties employing some twenty to twenty-five professional cricketers, a total perhaps of some 450 people to whom the selectors could offer their largesse. Cricketers would make runs or take wickets and be noted at a distance in a Lord's committee room and offered a Test match on the strength of one or two good county performances or games against touring sides which were often below Test match strength, because their stars were resting. It was even said, at one time, that the Australians were inclined to feed runs to batsmen whom they sought to see selected by England because they knew how to deal with them in the Test match arena. If those selected by England's selectors failed to reproduce their county performances they were summarily dropped and, quite frankly, forgotten. If they later enjoyed an upsurge they might be lucky enough to be resurrected and given another game or two. Nearly sixty of them have had only one or two Tests before passing into oblivion. If you add in those with three or four caps you are into the nervous nineties. John Stephenson, once of Essex and now of Hampshire, even thought it worthwhile to establish a club for the unfortunates. There was never any question of seeing whether a player had that extra special ability that might make him a Test match bowler or batsman and no reason was ever given as to why someone had been selected or discarded. Players have to accept the selectors' judgement in the same way as they accept the umpire's decision on the field. But there is a difference. One decision is part of a game and must be accepted, otherwise chaos would result. The other relates to a man's career and how he and his family may prosper, in short, how his life may develop. Many professional cricketers have related to the author how they have heard of their selection or omission from the Test side by turning on their radio as they drove to a Sunday League match or hearing from the car park attendant when they arrived at the ground. It is almost unbelievable, but it is true.

At the start of the 1999 Test series against New Zealand, following England's disastrous exit from the World Cup, England's selectors appeared to be ready with bold decisions. Alec Stewart, who had been asked to take on the almost impossible task of leading batsman, wicketkeeper and captain, was summarily dismissed and Nasser Hussain appointed in his stead. Chris Read, Nottinghamshire's young wicketkeeper, batsmen Aftab Habib and Darren Maddy from Leicestershire and the fast bowlers Alex Tudor from Surrey and Ed Giddins from Warwickshire, all found themselves promoted to Test match status. All well and good, one might have throught. For the South Africa tour in the winter of 1999/2000 further new names appeared. Michael Vaughan, the Yorkshire batsman who had led an 'A' tour with distinction, Chris Adams, the Sussex captain, Gavin Hamilton, the Yorkshire all-rounder who had performed well for Scotland in the World Cup, and Graeme Swann, the Northants off-spinning all-rounder were all in the party. Only Vaughan looks like succeeding. The others, like so many England aspirants before them, have disappeared as though they had never existed.

At the start of the 2000 season, the English and Wales Cricket Board under the leadership of Lord MacLaurin and its Chief Executive, Tim Lamb, had the wisdom and foresight to promote the concept of a Test match squad. Central contracts are nowadays the order of the day and are being accepted, in some cases reluctantly, by the counties, who nevertheless draw much of their income from Test match receipts. The idea makes sense because, of the multitude of county cricketers theoretically available for selection by England, only a small percentage are ever likely to reach Test standard. The selected few will be able to meet and train together and, playing rather less cricket than hitherto, save some of their energy for the Test match arena. It all seems to make sense, but the reality is, however, very different. The twelve centrally contracted players were presumably to be the basis of England's Test team. Most people might have thought that twelve was rather too few to form a viable squad. Now one has withdrawn through injury and two others appear already to have been discarded, one probably for good. While horses must be picked for courses, with allowances made for slight changes to counter injury problems or when some pitches require an extra spinner or batsman, it would be a great shame if England's selectors were to have returned once more to their old 'pick and mix' ways. Did they think hard enough before advising the ECB who the contracted players should be? England's success in the 2000/01 winter and a wiser selection of contracted players perhaps indicates that some lessons have finally been learned.

Wayne Larkins was a prime example of a cricketer of great ability who was not singled out at the right time and, when he was finally selected, was not given any length of time to settle himself into the Test team. He was the victim of an impoverished system. It is instructive to note that Wayne played twelve of his thirteen Tests against Australia or the West Indies. It may not be true nowadays, but in the last twenty years there have been times when Tests against New Zealand, India (in England) and even Pakistan have been relatively soft options, but he had just the one match against India and, in any case, that was in the sub-continent. These sides are not soft options any longer, because all Test playing countries except England, Zimbabwe and perhaps Bangladesh have organised a domestic set-up that provides for real competition and gives the opportunity for Test players to play against worthy opposition in the domestic field. Wayne Larkins ended his thirteen-Test international batting career with 493 runs at an average of 20.54 and his 25 one-day international appearances produced 591 runs at an average of 24.62. These are relatively insignificant sets of statistics, but his record also includes one of three or four really great innings played for England in one-day internationals, namely, his 124 against Australia in Hyderabad in 1989.

So is Wayne Larkins' failure to become a really great Test match batsman, as Richard Peel has suggested he should have been, all the fault of poor English selection and organisation? Well, of course, a large part of it is, but it cannot be the whole answer. Geoff Cook has wisely pointed out that success at domestic level can normally be seen as 90 per cent ability and 10 per cent 'bottle'. At Test level he believes the percentages to be nearer 60 per cent and 40 per cent. Is this then where Wayne Larkins went wrong? Well, maybe. But again, it is not the whole story. Wayne is known as an after-match drinker – as Allan Lamb has said, 'When it came down to having a few pints then Ned would be in the 'A' team' – but he never touches a drop during the day when he is playing in a match. Was any attempt made to help him to understand his responsibilities when he first went on tour to Australia in 1979? None at all, it would seem. He thought that he was going on tour as the reserve opener, but when a vacancy occurred, another player – not an opener – was preferred. Small wonder perhaps that he spent too much time in the amusement arcades of Sydney and Melbourne. Small wonder, too, that he drank cans of beer on top of the scoreboard when he should have been paying more attention to the cricket.

In this context it is interesting to note what happened recently to Ricky Ponting, the Australian batsman. Having drunk far beyond his limit, he became involved in a brawl in an Australian pub. It certainly brought discredit on the Australian Test team, so he was severely reprimanded by the Australian Cricket Board and given a ban for some matches. He was not dropped without a word; on the contrary, a fair number of words were spoken in his direction. It has now been announced that he is in line, at a minimum, for the Australian vice-captaincy because it is recognised that he has an above-average cricket brain and will help Australia to maintain its high cricketing standards. Although Adam Gilchrist has for the moment beaten him to the job since Shane Warne's dismissal for inappropriate behaviour, his time will almost certainly come one day. Could anything so positive happen in England? One hopes that, nowadays, it might be the case, but the jury is still out.

Wayne Larkins once said to the author: 'The only thing that I do well in life is play cricket.' This is hardly a dreadful thing to say, but he has allowed events to overtake him. Cricketers in general do not believe, as Wayne has apparently done, that life is just one long innings. The well-educated and those who are street-wise and possess drive find posts as correpondents or commentators, those who feel they cannot give up the 'hands-on' way of life become first-class umpires or coaches of international sides or, less ambitiously, school or club sides; some are quite content to take on lesser posts such as running the club shop.

Wayne has done none of these things. If he had had his due as England Test player, he might have entered different avenues. Sadly, that has not come about. He has just wanted to bat on until the close of play. I, for one, still relish watching his great 172 at Wardown Park; many others, around county grounds, would still love to see him at his outrageously fluent best. But it is an era that is almost over; at best you can see him now on some Minor Counties ground. *Sic transeat gloria.* He will be hugely missed by many spectators. And what will he be left with? Some magnificent memories, but a future about as clear as Hove cricket ground when the sea fret comes in.

Wayne enjoys some liquid refreshment while playing in the benefit match for Malcolm Marshall's son at the HAC ground in August 2000. (Graham Morris)

WAYNE LARKINS IN STATISTICS

BATTING RECORD

	M	I	N.O.	R	H.S.	AV	100/50	CT
For England (Tests 1979-91)	13	25	1	493	64	20.54	-/3	8
For England (One-day internationals 1979-91)	25	24	0	591	124	24.62	1/-	8
For England First class touring 1979-91	11	21	2	574	124★	30.21	2/1	5

For Northamptonshire (1972-91)

	M	I	N.O.	R	H.S.	AV	100/50	CT
First class	363	628	43	20,317	252	34.73	44/85	213
Gillette/Natwest	44	43	3	1,436	121★	35.90	1/11	19
Benson & Hedges Cup	70	66	3	2,088	132	33.14	5/8	14
Sunday League	238	229	13	6,068	172★	28.09	10/31	70

For Durham (1992-95)

	M	I	N.O.	R	H.S.	AV	100/50	CT
First class	67	120	6	4,278	158★	37.53	10/20	61
Natwest	8	8	0	337	113	42.13	1/1	2
Benson & Hedges Cup	12	12	1	572	123	52.00	2/3	7
Sunday League	50	48	5	1405	131★	32.67	4/4	21

All First Class Matches

Career Total	482	842	54	27,142	252	34.44	59/116	306

All Gillette/Natwest, Benson & Hedges, Sunday League (for Northants and Durham)

Gillette/Natwest	52	51	3	1,773	121*	36.93	2/12	21
Benson & Hedges	82	78	4	2,660	132	35.94	7/11	21
Sunday League	290	278	18	7,499	172*	28.84	14/36	91
Career Total	424	407	25	11,932	172*	31.23	23/59	133

First Class Hundreds (59)

1973	109	Northants v. Cambridge University, Fenners
1975	127	Northants v. Essex, Chelmsford
1976	167	Northants v. Warwickshire, Edgbaston
1977	110	Northants v. Yorkshire, Bradford
	103*	Northants v. Kent, Northampton
1978	170*	Northants v. Worcestershire, Northampton
	118	Northants v. Yorkshire, Harrogate
	107	Northants v. Nottinghamshire, Northampton
1979	136	Northants v. Middlesex, Northampton
	115	Northants v. Leicestershire, Wellingborough
	103	Northants v. Kent, Northampton
1980	156	Northants v. Leicestershire, Leicester
	127	Northants v. Gloucestershire, Northampton
	105	Northants v. Hampshire, Wellingbrough
	103*	Northants v. Glamorgan, Cardiff
1981	157	Northants v. Warwickshire, Edgbaston
	130	Northants v. Warwickshire, Northampton
	126	Northants v. Derbyshire, Derby
	117	Northants v. Cambridge University, Fenners
1982	186	Northants v. Yorkshire, Middlesbrough
	137	Northants v. Somerset, Northampton
	118*	Northants v. Yorkshire, Northampton
	110*	Northants v. Worcestershire, Northampton
	105	Northants v. Derbyshire, Northampton
1983	252	Northants v. Glamorgan, Cardiff
	236	Northants v. Derbyshire, Derby
	187	Northants v. Lancashire, Northampton
	145	Northants v. Glamorgan, Northampton
	100	Northants v. Middlesex, Lord's
1983-84	116	Eastern Province v. Natal, Port Elizabeth

	110	Eastern Province *v.* Western Province, Cape Town
1984	183★	Northants *v.* Sussex, Northampton
	151	Northants *v.* Lancashire, Northampton
	108	Northants *v.* Somerset, Northampton
1985	163	Northants *v.* Worcestershire, Worcester
	140	Northants *v.* Nottinghamshire, Northampton
	117	Northants *v.* Surrey, Northampton
1987	120	Northants *v.* Hampshire, Southampton
	115	Northants *v.* Worcestershire, Northampton
	101★	Northants *v.* Yorkshire, Northampton
1988	134	Northants *v.* Gloucestershire, Bristol
	112★	Northants *v.* Kent, Northampton
1989	126	Northants *v.* Oxford University, Oxford
	116	Northants *v.* Kent, Maidstone
	108	MCC *v.* Michael Parkinson's World XI, Scarborough
1989-90	124★	England XI *v.* Jamaica, Kingston
	107	England XI *v.* Leeward Islands, St Kitts
1990	207	Northants *v.* Essex, Northampton
	107	Northants *v.* Surrey, The Oval
1992	143	Durham *v.* Glamorgan, Cardiff
	140	Durham *v.* Glamorgan, Hartlepool
	118	Durham *v.* Pakistani Touring Team, Chester-le-Street
	117	Durham *v.* Somerset, Taunton
1993	151	Durham *v.* Australian Touring Team, Durham University
	113★	Durham *v.* Warwickshire, Darlington
	106	Durham *v.* Sussex, Durham University
1994	158★	Durham *v.* Gloucestershire, Gateshead Fell
1995	121	Durham *v.* Nottinghamshire, Chester-le-Street
	112	Durham *v.* Northants, Northampton#

This innings completed the 'full set' against First Class Counties

One-Day Hundreds (24)

1978	107★	Northants *v.* Surrey, Tring (SL)
1979	111	Northants *v.* Leicestershire, Wellingborough (SL)
1980	108	Northants *v.* Warwickshire, Edgbaston (B&H)#
1982	158	Northants *v.* Worcestershire, Luton (SL)
	132	Northants *v.* Warwickshire, Edgbaston (B&H)#
	126	Northants *v.* Scotland, Glasgow (B&H)#
1983	172★	Northants *v.* Worcestershire, Luton (SL)
	102	Northants *v.* Gloucestershire, Northampton (SL)
1985	126	Northants *v.* Surrey, Guildford (SL)
	105	Northants *v.* Scotland, Northampton (B&H)#
1987	121★	Northants *v.* Essex (Chelmsford) (NW)$
1989	101	Northants *v.* Gloucestershire, Moreton-in-Marsh (SL)

1989-90	124	England *v.* Australia, Hyderabad (Nehru Cup)$
1990	111	Northants *v.* Scotland, Northampton (B&H)
	109	Northants *v.* Gloucestershire, Northampton (SL)
	104	Northants *v.* Lancashire, Northampton (SL)
1991	108	Northants *v.* Essex, Northampton (SL)
1992	113	Durham *v.* Ireland, Dublin (NW)
1993	128	Durham *v.* Nottinghamshire, Chester-le-Street (SL)
	114	Durham *v.* Yorkshire, Headingley (SL)
	110★	Durham *v.* Hampshire, Stockton-on-Tess (B&H)#
1994	131★	Durham *v.* Hampshire, Portsmouth (SL)
	108	Durham *v.* Northants, Hartlepool (S)
1995	123	Durham *v.* Minor Counties, Jesmond (B&H)#

NW=Natwest Trophy B&H=Benson and Hedges Cup SL=Sunday League
(John Player, Refuge Assurance or Axa Equity and Law)
= Benson and Hedges Gold Award $ = Natwest Man of the Match

BOWLING RECORD

	Balls	Runs	Wickets	Avge	Best	5wI
First class	3517	1915	42	45.59	5-59	1
ODI	15	22	0	-	-	-
Gillette/Natwest	455	274	4	68.50	2-38	-
Benson & Hedges	675	444	16	27.75	4-37	-
Sunday League	2033	1679	57	29.45	5-32	1
All non-ODI one day	3163	2397	77	31.13	5-32	2

RECORDS

At time of first-class retirement in 1995

Sunday League	Most hundreds (14)
	Second most runs (7,499) (G.A. Gooch = 8,359)
	Third highest score (172★) (G.A. Gooch 176, I.T. Botham 175★)
Benson & Hedges	Fifth most runs (2,660) (G.A. Gooch 4,934,
	M.W. Gatting 2,776, C.J. Tavaré 2,761,
	D.W. Randall 2,663)
	Second most hundreds (7) (G.A. Gooch 14, G.A.Hick 7)

PLAYERS ON AND OFF THE FIELD

Keith ('KV') Andrew: Born 1929. England wicketkeeper and captain of Northants 1962-66, who threatened to resign from the County Committee and take Wayne Larkins to Lancashire if the latter was not retained after the 1974 season.

Dennis Brookes, JP: Born 1915. Grand old man of Northants cricket, opening batsman, captain, coach and president of the County Cricket Club. First mentor and coach to Wayne Larkins, believing that his technique was near perfect at the age of sixteen.

David Capel: Born 1963. All-rounder. Northants 1981-98. 15 Tests and 23 one-day internationals. Scored 12,202 first class runs and took 546 first-class wickets. Highest score: 175 Northants *v.* Leicestershire 1995. Best bowling 7-44 Northants *v.* Warwickshire 1995-1999. Northants Director of Youth Cricket. Great supporter and admirer of Wayne Larkins.

Geoff Cook: Born 1951. Opening batsman. Northants 1971-90, County Captain 1981-88, played in 7 Tests. From 1991 to date: Director of Cricket for Durham County Cricket Club. Scored 23,277 first-class runs. Highest score: 203 Northants *v.* Yorkshire, 1988. Wayne Larkins' opening partner 1978-89. Was sad to have to announce Wayne's release from Durham at the end of the 1995 season.

Nick Cook: Born 1956. Slow left-arm bowler. Leicestershire 1978-85. Northants 1986-94. 15 Tests. Took 879 first-class wickets. Remains on Northants coaching staff. Candidate for Northants captaincy with Wayne Larkins and Allan Lamb in 1989.

Graham Gooch: Born 1953. Opening batsman, medium-pace bowler and legendary England cricketer. Mentor and great friend to Wayne Larkins. Essex 1973-1997. County Captain 1986-87 and 1989-94. England 1975-95. Played in 118 Tests (34 as captain) and 125 one-day internationals. Scored 44,841 first-class runs and 128 centuries. Highest score: 333 England *v.*India 1990. Best bowling: 7-14 Essex *v.* Worcestershire 1982. First met Wayne in the late 1960s in an Essex *v.* Huntingdonshire junior match, when Graham was keeping wicket and batting at number eleven. Captained Wayne on three tours: 1982 'rebel' tour to South Africa, England tours to West Indies in 1989-90 and to Australia in 1990-91. Latterly England selector and batting coach.

Gordon Greenidge: Born 1951. Outstanding West Indian opening batsman whom Wayne Larkins sought to emulate. Hampshire 1970-1987. Played 108 Tests for West Indies 1974-1990, scoring 7,558 runs.

Michael Green: Journalist and one-time captain of Bedford Town Second XI, who while batting with Wayne Larkins, advised him to play for a draw but was surprised when the precocious thirteen-year-old flayed the opposition bowling to the tune of 74 not out and won the game for his side.

Alan Hodgson: Born 1951. Northants 1970-79. Fast-medium bowler who handed over the duties of youngest professional on the staff to Wayne Larkins and who received his county cap from Mushtaq Mohammad on the same day in 1976 as Wayne.

David Hoare: Vice-chairman, secretary and former player of Bedfordshire County Cricket Club who was instrumental in bringing Wayne Larkins to Minor Counties cricket at the end of his first-class career in 1995.

Simon Hughes: Born 1959. Former Middlesex and Durham fast-medium bowler who batted with Wayne Larkins during the 'piece of piss' episode with Leicestershire fast bowler, David Millns. Now a cricket correspondent and author of several successful cricket books.

Allan Lamb: Born 1954. South African batsman of high ability who qualified to play for England. Northants 1978-95 (County Captain 1989-95). Played in 79 Tests and 122 one-day internationals. Scored 32,502 first-class runs and 89 hundreds. Highest score: 294 for Orange Free State *v.* Eastern Province 1987-88. Beat Wayne Larkins for the Northants captaincy in 1989.

Tim Lamb: Born 1953. Medium-fast bowler. Middlesex 1974-1977. Northants 1978-83. From 1997 to date: Chief Executive of the England and Wales Cricket Board. Keen observer of Wayne Larkins as a team member.

Jane Larkins (née Faulkner). Wayne Larkins' wife. A secretary for the solicitors Shoosmith and Harrison, she met Wayne at a disco at Northants County Cricket ground in the early 1970s, married him in 1975 and is the mother of his two daughters, Philippa and Amy. Divorced Wayne in the late 1980s.

Mavis Larkins: Died 1998. Wayne Larkins' mother and a keen supporter of her son and Northants cricket, whose sitting room was decorated with photos of her famous son.

Debbie Lines: Wayne Larkins' companion since 1988. Met Wayne at a party at Ian Botham's farmhouse in 1987 when he frolicked on the dance floor wearing the host's fishing outfit.

Mushtaq Mohammad: Born 1943. Famous Pakistani Test cricketer, captain of Northants in 1976/77, who had a great affection for Wayne Larkins and a great belief in his ability. Caused some dismay in his own team when he failed to discipline Wayne for his late arrival at Worcester in 1977 and his subsequent failure to attend the team talk.

Richard Peel: Cricket journalist at the *Chronicle and Echo* in Northampton, subsequently ECB Director of Public Relations and now ITV's Director of Publicity. Counted the rounds while he and Wayne Larkins each drank fifteen pints after the

Glamorgan match in 1983 and staggered to his hotel room as Wayne went into the bar for two glasses of brandy.

George Sharp: Born 1950. Wicketkeeper and middle-order batsman. Northants 1967-85. Took 565 first-class catches and made 90 first-class stumpings. First-class umpire 1991 to date. International umpire 1996 to date. Summoned Wayne Larkins by phone from his slumbers at the Gifford Hotel, Worcester, at 10.45 a.m. in July 1977.

David Steele: Born 1941. Solid and resourceful batsman who wished that he had had half of Wayne Larkins' batting ability. Northants 1963-78 and 1982-84. Derbyshire 1979 (county captain). Scored 22,346 first-class runs and played eight Tests for England in 1975-76 when he batted heroically against the Australians Lillee and Thomson and the West Indian fast-bowlers. Claims credit for giving Wayne the name 'Ned' at Northants County Cricket Club.

Ken Turner: Legendary tough secretary of Northants County Cricket Club who hounded Wayne Larkins when he was a young professional, but was instrumental in saving him from dismissal at the end of the 1974 season. Was virulent in his disapproval of Wayne's 'rebel' tour to South Africa.

P. J. (Jim) Watts: Born 1940. Cheshire headmaster who captained Northants for much of the 1970s and persuaded Wayne Larkins to start opening the innings. Made Wayne face up to the pressures of first-class cricket, but chided him for joining the 1982 'rebel' tour to South Africa.

Peter Willey: Born 1949. All-rounder. Northants 1966-83. Leicestershire 1984-90 (captain 1987). Scored 24,361 first-class runs and took 756 first-class wickets. Run out by Wayne Larkins at the end of his highest score: 227 Northants *v.* Somerset 1976. Best bowling 7-37 Northants v. Oxford University 1975. 26 Tests and 26 ODIs. First-class umpire 1993 to date. International umpire 1996 to date. Wayne's room-mate for much of their careers together. Together with Wayne the recipient of 2,016 pints of beer from Northampton brewery as a reward for their efforts in Australia 1979/80.

David Wilson: Schoolmaster and cricket coach in Huntingdon who first noticed Wayne Larkins' precocious ability and brought him into representative junior sides. Was impressed by Wayne's kindness when he presented him with an autographed miniature bat after the 1979 World Cup Final at Lord's.

BIBLIOGRAPHY

Wisden Cricketers' Almanack (1972-2000)

The Playfair Cricket Annual (1972-2000)

The Cricketer (relevant editions)

Wisden Cricket Monthly (relevant editions)

Northamptonshire County Cricket Club Yearbooks (1972-1992)

The Cricketers' Who's Who (several editions) (Queen Anne Press)

Jack Bannister: *The Innings of my Life* (Headline 1993)

Simon Barnes: *Phil Edmonds - a Singular Man* (The Kingswood Press 1986)

Ian Botham: *The Botham Report* (Collins Willow 1997)

Mike Brearley: *The Art of Captaincy* (Hodder and Stoughton 1985)

Ralph Dellor: *Durham: Birth of a First-Class County* (Bloomsbury 1992)

Matthew Engel and Andrew Radd: *The History of Northamptonshire County Cricket Club* (Christopher Helm 1993)

Richard Evans: *The Ultimate Test* (Partridge Press 1990)

Bill Frindall: *The Wisden Book of Test Cricket* (two volumes) (Macdonald and Jane's 1979 and 1990)

Bill Frindall and Victor Isaacs: *The Wisden Book of One-Day International Cricket* (John Wisden 1985)

Graham Gooch (with Alan Lee): *Out of the Wilderness* (Willow Books 1985)

Graham Gooch (with Patrick Murphy): *Captaincy* (Stanley Paul 1992)

Graham Gooch (with Frank Keating): *My Autobiography* (Collins Willow 1995)

Simon Hughes: *From Minor to Major* (Hodder and Stoughton 1992)

Simon Hughes: *A Lot of Hard Yakka* (Headline 1997)

Allan Lamb: *My Autobiography* (Collins Willow 1997)

Christopher Martin-Jenkins: *World Cricketers* (OUP 1996)

Geoffrey Moorhouse: *The Best Loved Game* (Hodder and Stoughton 1979)

David Norrie: *Athers* (Pelham Books 1997)

Neville Scott and Nick Cook: *England Test Cricket - The Years of Indecision* (The Kingswood Press 1992)

Allen Synge: *Sins of Omission* (Headline 1997)

Ivo Tennant: *Graham Gooch* (Witherby 1992)

Phil Tufnell: *My Autobiography* (Collins Willow 1999)

INDEX